D1238627

THE CATHOLIC BIBLICAL QUARTERLY MONOGRAPH SERIES

4

FROM CANAAN TO EGYPT

STRUCTURAL AND THEOLOGICAL CONTEXT FOR THE JOSEPH STORY

FROM CANAAN TO EGYPT

STRUCTURAL AND THEOLOGICAL CONTEXT
FOR THE JOSEPH STORY

George W. Coats

Lexington Theological Seminary
Lexington, Kentucky

The Catholic Biblical Association of America
Washington, D.C. 20064
1976

FROM CANAAN TO EGYPT
STRUCTURAL AND THEOLOGICAL CONTEXT FOR THE
JOSEPH STORY
by George W. Coats

© 1976 The Catholic Biblical Association of America
Washington, D.C.

Grateful acknowledgment is made for permission to quote from the following works:

Gerhard von Rad, *Genesis, A Commentary*. Copyright 1961, W. L. Jenkins.
Copyright SCM Press, Ltd., 1972. Used by Permission of The Westminister Press.

Martin Noth, *A History of Pentateuchal Traditions,* translated by Bernhard W.
Anderson, (c) 1972. Used by permission of Prentice-Hall, Inc., Englewood Cliffs, N.J.

D. B. Redford, *A Study of the Biblical Story of Joseph (Genesis 37–50)*
(*VTSup* 20). Used by permission of E. J. Brill, Publishers, Leiden.

PRODUCED IN THE UNITED STATES

LIBRARY OF CONGRESS CATALOGUE CARD NUMBER: 75-11382
ISBN 0-915170-03-5

GERHARD von RAD
In Memory
of friendship beyond the call of hospitality

CLAUS WESTERMANN
In Appreciation
for friendship past and future

TABLE OF CONTENTS

ACKNOWLEDGEMENTS

I am indebted to Professors Gerhard von Rad and Claus Westermann, of the University of Heidelberg, Germany, for reading the entire manuscript and generously offering time for discussing particular items of exegesis, and to Professors J. L. Crenshaw of Vanderbilt University and W. Lee Humphreys of the University of Tennessee for their critical comments on various stages of the manuscript production. Moreover, my colleague at Lexington Theological Seminary, Professor David P. Polk, has contributed immeasurably to the mix of seminars, private discussions, and formal, public responses that was formative in my own work on the Joseph story. These men have shown me qualities in the Joseph story that could not have been discovered in isolated study. They have shared my joy with this masterpiece of narrative art. But they do not bear responsibility for the limitations in my conclusions about its character.

I am also indebted to Monsignor Patrick W. Skehan, the former chairman of the *CBQMS* Editorial Board, under whose administration this monograph was accepted for the series, and to his efficient colleagues. Their care in evaluating my manuscript and particularly their perceptive suggestions for various improvements have contributed to the prospects for quality and effective communication in the work. Needless to say, however, they, too, do not bear responsibility for the deficiencies that remain.

For moral and financial support during a sabbatical leave from my responsibilities in the classroom, I would express my gratitude to the faculty and staff of the Lexington Theological Seminary, Lexington, Kentucky. For election as Stipendiat and the corresponding financial support for research with the faculty of the University in Heidelberg, I would also thank the staff of the Alexander von Humboldt Stiftung, Bad Godesberg, Germany. Through patience and hard labor in typing and retyping, the secretarial staff of the Seminary has won my lasting appreciation. And finally, to my wife, Sandy, and my son, Andrew, for interest and support in hours of conversation about Joseph during a year of life in Heidelberg, and to my daughter, Charissa, our flower from Heidelberg, I can think of nothing adequate enough to say . . . except thanks.

INTRODUCTION

Traditions about Israel's early history, preserved particularly in the Pentateuch—Hexateuch as narratives, divide into five distinct groups: 1) patriarchal traditions, 2) exodus traditions, 3) traditions about Israel's life in the wilderness, 4) the Sinai complex of legal and narrative traditions, and finally 5) the conquest traditions. These groups, however, reflect more than historical organization. They constitute, at least in part, the result of theological reflection, a canonical scheme for Israel's basic theological confessions. In the traditions about the patriarchal period, for example, Israel remembers God's promise for a great progeny and possession of a great land, as well as his commission to bring blessing to the nations. In the exodus traditions, Israel celebrates God's response to her cries under the burden of Egyptian oppression. In the wilderness narratives, the focal point centers on God's leading Israel through a great and terrible wilderness, protecting his people from the dangers of hunger and thirst and the threat of enemies. The Sinai complex comprises the law God gave Israel on the sacred mountain, as well as narrative traditions associated with the law. And finally, in the conquest theme, Israel remembers that God led his people triumphantly across the Jordan as the Canaanites fled in panic.

This collection of traditions does not, however, derive from one single act of theological reflection about Israel's early history. At least three problems suggest that it was formulated over an extended period of transmission from generation to generation.[1] The first one lies in the relationship between the Sinai traditions and the other major themes. The Sinai complex may derive from a completely distinct cultic group, originally unrelated to the people who remembered the exodus and the wilderness. It may be closely related to the exodus traditions, the natural consequence of implications in the exodus event itself.[2] It may be a part of the wilderness collection of traditions, one complex among several set within the scope of the wilderness itinerary.[3] The relationship is not yet clear. But whatever the relationship, it remains certain that a basic theological assertion can be seen through the traditions about Sinai: God gave his law to his people. And perhaps the most basic law in the complex defines the relationship between God and his people: "You shall have no other gods before me."

A second problem lies in the position of the primeval history for the fivefold structure of the Pentateuch—Hexateuch. No evidence suggests that as

---

[1] Gerhard von Rad, *Genesis, a Commentary* (revised edition; Philadelphia: Westminster, 1972) 13–23.

[2] A. Weiser, *The Old Testament: Its Formation and Development* (New York: Association, 1961) 81–99. For more recent literature, cf. H. Gese, "Bemerkungen zur Sinaitradition," *ZAW* 79 (1967) 137–154.

[3] George W. Coats, "The Wilderness Itinerary," *CBQ* 34 (1972) 135–152.

an element in the skein of Israel's theological traditions the primeval history is older than the oldest literary source. It may serve as a theological foundation for the Yahwist's distinctive view of the patriarchal promise. At least it is clear that in the primeval history the scope of interest encompasses the entire spectrum of mankind rather than the limited world view of a single people. And the story of the single people begins in the light of that spectrum.[4]

The third problem appears in the patriarchal promise for possession of a great land. The promise anticipates immediate fulfillment. But fulfillment does not occur so promptly. The promise—fulfillment framework has been broken apart for the sake of the exodus—wilderness traditions. And indeed, fulfillment of the promise does not appear to capture any part of the Yahwist's (or even the priestly) narration. Insofar as the major sources of the Pentateuch are concerned, the conquest traditions are missing. The promise orients toward the future. Its fulfillment is latent in the exodus and wilderness narrations. But the fulfillment never appears as a fully developed theme of narration, at least not in the context of the Pentateuch.[5]

It is just at this juncture of the third problem that the Joseph story demands attention. The patriarchal traditions presuppose the life of a family, or perhaps better, the life of tribal groups in Canaan. They reveal evidence of an important theological foundation stone: God promised the fathers possession of the land. But the narration breaks. The scene changes. The exodus traditions do not set the principals of narration in Canaan, ready to receive the land. To the contrary, they are in Egypt, the slaves of the Pharaoh. The Joseph story fits into that gap. But how? It is clear that the Joseph story is not simply one more saga in the collection of traditions about the patriarchs. In both structure and genre, the Joseph story is distinct from the stories that make up the substance of narration from Genesis 12 through 36. It is also clear that the Joseph story does not fit into the narration of the exodus theme. Where, then, does it belong? Is it a story that had its own original life to live, quite apart from the gap in structure it fits into? Does it develop its own unique theological affirmations, quite apart from the classical assertions reflected in the canonical structure of the Pentateuch? Is it, in effect, completely isolated from its context, secondarily placed into its present position as a stop-gap measure? Or does it have intrinsic relationships with its context? Does it show structural or theological relationships with the rest of the Pentateuch? The thesis of this monograph is that while the story develops distinctive themes in its own right, the constituent themes in the story reveal indispensable functions that derive from the context.

[4] H. W. Wolff, "The Kerygma of the Yahwist," *Int* 20 (1966) 131–158. Cf. also W. Malcolm Clark, "The Flood and the Structure of the Pre-patriarchal History," *ZAW* 83 (1971) 184–210.

[5] For a different position on involvement in conquest tradition by J and P, cf. Sigmund Mowinckel, *Tetrateuch-Pentateuch-Hexateuch; die Berichte über die Landnahme in den drei alttestamentlichen Geschichtswerken* (*BZAW* 90; Berlin: Töpelmann, 1964) 9–32, 51–76.

I offer no extensive review of research on the Joseph story as a part of this introduction. Contributions to the discussion of the Joseph story with unique relevance to my argument will be evaluated in the course of the coming chapters. It is important, nonetheless, to sketch briefly the discussion that provides context for my work. An initial point of departure for the sketch, and a convenient point to cut into the discussion, is the provocative, programmatic work of Martin Noth.[6] He suggested that the Joseph story must be seen as a bridge between the patriarchs and the exodus. It would thus presuppose, not only the oral history of both themes, but the unification of the traditions as two stages in a canonical scheme. Indeed, Noth suggests that the story may have grown from the credo assertion that "Jacob and his sons went down to Egypt" (Jos 24:4). He observes: "How might that have come about? This question could well have stimulated the imaginative power of gifted narrators; and thus there developed, through the use of general narrative motifs, the extensive and charming structure of the transmitted Joseph story."[7] Moreover, as a bridge piece, the Joseph story would be rather late in the history of Pentateuchal traditions and reflect a tradition history that is quite different from the history of the patriarchal traditions.

Significantly, Noth does not emphasize any other structural function for the Joseph story than its function as a bridge over the wide gap between Canaan and Egypt. But neither does he define exactly how the Joseph story fulfills that bridge function. Obvious discontinuities, particularly in genre and tradition history, distinguish the Joseph story from the patriarchal traditions, as well as the exodus narration. But elements of continuity are also present. And those continuities and their opposing poles of discontinuities he does not evaluate in assigning the Joseph story a bridge role.

Gerhard von Rad contributed the next principal stage in the discussion.[8] Von Rad's sensitivity to the artistic structure of the Joseph story cannot be surpassed.[9] Points from his discussion of structure and style will be incorporated into my analysis in the first chapter. Here it is important to note von Rad's contribution to the question of context. The Joseph story, according to von Rad, breathes the air of wisdom. And as a consequence, it appears to have a marked contrast to the Pentateuchal context it appears in. Indeed, it

---

[6] Martin Noth, *A History of Pentateuchal Traditions* (tr. Bernhard W. Anderson; Englewood Cliffs: Prentice-Hall, 1972) 208–213. Cf. more recently, Odil H. Steck, *Die Paradieserzählung. Eine Auslegung von Genesis 2, 4b-3, 24* (*Biblische Studien* 60; Neukirchen: Neukirchener Verlag, 1970) 120, n. 291.

[7] Noth, p. 209.

[8] Gerhard von Rad, "The Joseph Narrative and Ancient Wisdom," *The Problem of the Hexateuch and other essays* (Edinburgh: Oliver and Boyd, 1966) 292–300. Cf. also Gerhard von Rad, *Die Josephsgeschichte* (*Biblische Studien* 5; Neukirchen: Neukirchener Verlag, 1964) 5–24.

[9] Cf. also R. Hals, *The Theology of the Book of Ruth* (*Facet Books, Biblical Series* 23; Philadelphia: Fortress, 1969) 34–44.

seems to be important for von Rad's argument to show that as a piece of literature developed from the womb of wisdom, the Joseph story has no roots in the classical theological traditions of the Pentateuch. It would not be isolated from the Old Testament generally, since wisdom literature, and literature influenced by wisdom, can be detected in increasingly larger portions of the Old Testament. But its position in the Pentateuch as a bridge between the patriarchs and the exodus would represent a secondary function imposed on the Joseph story when it was incorporated into the final form of the text.

More recently D. B. Redford has brought his skill as a specialist in Egyptology to bear on arguments about the origin of the Joseph story.[10] With his contribution in view, it is now impossible to consider seriously any suggestions about a direct historical line from the story to the Egyptian court of the Ramesside period. Redford adds, moreover, to a positive evaluation of the stylistic elements in the Joseph story narration. He differs sharply from both Noth and von Rad, however, in describing the relationship of the Joseph story to its context. For Redford, the Joseph story is entirely isolated. It has no theological character relevant for the dominant categories of organization in Pentateuchal theology; and no contact with wisdom. And that isolation represents an advantage: "Except for chapter 39, 'god' is heard only on the lips of the characters in the story; the writer eschews the tedious, moralizing commentary which clutters so much of holy writ."[11] The point is made more explicitly in a summary:

> "The theological outlook of the writer of Gen 37–50 is different from that of the Patriarchal narrator. He does not mention the Covenant or the Promise, ubiquitous in the earlier chapters of Genesis. He is not interested in supplying the reader with comment on matters theological, as the Patriarchal author was. In fact, with the glaring exception of chapter 39, the writer nowhere uses YHWH, and when 'elōhîm is used it is always in the direct speech of the characters of the story. He lets the story convey his message without trying to ram it down the readers' throats at every turn of the plot."[12]

Yet, a question remains. If the story originated as a work of art so completely isolated from the context it now appears in, how did it find its way to its present position in the Pentateuch? Redford would agree that in the final form of the text the story has a bridging role. But he feels that such a function would be too pedestrian to constitute an original characteristic of the story.[13] If, however, the story is so completely isolated from its context, why would it have been a convenient piece of literature to serve this stop-gap position?

---

[10] D. B. Redford, *A Study of the Biblical Story of Joseph (Genesis 37–50)* (*VTSup* 20; Leiden: Brill, 1970).
[11] Redford, p. 86.
[12] Redford, p. 247.
[13] Redford, p. 27.

This monograph thus orients around the overarching question of context for the Joseph story.[14] Its chapters focus specifically on structural and theological context. Its goal is to illumine the unique position of the Joseph story in the Pentateuch, yet to explore whether the story has any firm rootage in Pentateuchal theology that would undergird its position.

---

[14] H. Gunkel, *Genesis* (*HKAT* I. 1; 6th ed.; Göttingen: Vandenhoeck & Ruprecht, 1964) 395–401. E. A. Speiser, *Genesis* (*AB* 1; New York: Doubleday, 1964) 292–294.

CHAPTER 1

STRUCTURE AND UNITY IN THE JOSEPH STORY

Gerhard von Rad described the artistic characteristics of the Joseph story with effective insight, sensitive to both the literary standards for narratives in general and the peculiarities of the Joseph story in particular.[1] D. B. Redford expanded that description, again with effective insight, by noting especially that the Joseph story builds its plot with careful attention for symmetry.[2] That symmetry employs, among other techniques, an interaction of extremes: the brothers and a weak Joseph set over against the brothers and a powerful Joseph; evidence for Joseph's death set over against evidence for Joseph's life; Joseph lost *vis à vis* Benjamin protected. And there are other structural motifs that contribute to plot symmetry: Joseph's robe (Gen 37//39//41), a prisoner unjustly confined (Gen 40//42), a sudden change of fortune (Gen 41//45). Moreover, the Joseph story reveals a broad range of literary devices: irony, simile, metaphor, double entendre, hyperbole. It deals with subtle emotions, like guilt, fear, despair. It leads the action of a scene to a point of crisis, then leaves that plot dangling while a new line of action develops, and then with deft strokes picks up the dangling ends. It controls the pace of action by retarding development of the plot, by recapitulation, by embellishment. These points have been satisfactorily discussed and need not be repeated here.

Yet, these observations do not exhaust an analysis of symmetry in the design of the story. How do such stylistic devices contribute to the development of a plot in this particular story? Do they in some manner reveal the basic goals of the story? Do they open any kind of evidence to clarify the relationship between the story and its context? Do they point to additional elements of symmetry in the composition of the story or in the relationship between the story and its context? Under the impetus of these questions, this chapter will seek to describe the structure of the Joseph story by analyzing the functional elements of the story's skeleton.

One word of caution, however, needs to be heard at just this point. The plan for my work calls first of all for an examination of structure in the story as it was preserved in the MT. Only after the functional unity of the story at this stage in its history has been defined can questions about literary sources

[1] Von Rad, *Die Josephsgeschichte*, pp. 5–24.

[2] Redford, pp. 66–105, 139–177. For comments particularly about the role of paradox in the structure of the Joseph story, cf. Donald A. Seybold, "Paradox and Symmetry in the Joseph Narrative," in *Literary Interpretations of Biblical Narratives,* eds. Kenneth R. R. Gros Louis, James S. Ackerman, Thayer S. Warshaw (Nashville: Abingdon, 1974) 59–73.

behind the MT be legitimately raised. To reverse the procedure and begin with a division of the story into its component sources begs the question about structure and unity, both in the final form of the text and in the sources that may lie behind the final form.

The organization of this chapter follows the pattern of structure in the story as a whole.[3] The following outline describes that pattern:

  I.   Exposition (37:1–4)
  II. Complication (37:5–36)
  III. Digression (39–41)
  IV. Complication (42)
  V.   Denouement (43–45)
  VI. Conclusion (46:1–47:27)

I. EXPOSITION (Gen 37:1–4)

The Joseph story opens with a statement about Jacob's life in Canaan. The sentence is constructed with a 3.m.s. Qal imperfect *waw* consecutive from the verb *yšb,* "to dwell" (*wayyēšeb*), followed by the subject, Jacob, and *two* specifications of place. The principal noun in both place specifications is *'ereṣ,* "land," in both cases controlled by the preposition *bet,* in both cases followed in a construct bond by a definition of the land: *bᵉ'ereṣ mᵉgûrê 'ābîw bᵉ'ereṣ kᵉnā'an.* "Jacob dwelt in the land of his father's sojournings, in the land of Canaan."

This opening is then followed in vs. 2 by a stereotyped *toledoth* formula: *'elleh tōlᵉdôt ya'ăqōb.* "These are the generations of Jacob." The *toledoth* formula at just this position, however, is problematic. One could normally expect such a formula to appear at the beginning of a unit, or at least at its end (thus, cf. Gen 2:4; 5:1; 6:9; 10:1; 11:10; 11:27; 25:12,19; 36:1,9). In Gen 37:2, the formula appears in second position. Its position here may well be influenced by Gen 36:8–9.[4] 36:8 begins, like 37:1, with a statement about the life of the subject in a particular place. The verb is a 3.m.s. Qal imperfect *waw* consecutive from the verb *yšb,* "to dwell." The subject is Esau. And a specification of place follows. Although controlled by the preposition *bet,* the specification of place does not designate a land, *'ereṣ,* but the hill country of Se'ir *bᵉhar śē'îr.* "Esau dwelt in the hill country of Se'ir." But nevertheless, the construction is similar to Gen 37:1–2. And significantly, in 36:8b, "Esau

---

[3] George W. Coats, "Redactional Unity in Gen 37–50," *JBL* 93 (1974) 15–21. In that essay I argued for exclusion of Gen 50:15–21 from the primary structure of the Joseph story. I suggested as well that a framework narrative begins in Gen 47:28, thus pinpointing the conclusion of the Joseph story as Gen 47:27. It is, of course, clear that Gen 38 is not an intrinsic element in the Joseph story.

[4] So, Redford, p. 14.

is Edom," intervenes between this designation of Esau's dwelling place and a *toledoth* formula in vs. 9.

Yet, this parallel, significantly outside the formal structure of the Joseph story, does not fully explain the first two verses of the Joseph story exposition. Indeed, it does nothing more than suggest that a common narrative formula used for transitions, or for the beginning or ending of a narrative unit, appears in both places (cf. also Gen 4:16; 13:18; 19:30; 20:1; 21:20, 21; 22:19; 26:6, 17; 50:22; *et al.*). The formula in 37:1 has a more impressive parallel in 47:27a, the last sentence of the Joseph story. Again, the sentence begins with a 3.m.s. Qal imperfect *waw* consecutive from the verb *yšb*, "to dwell." The subject follows. In this case, the subject is Israel rather than Jacob. But at least it is clear that the formula intends the same principal in the Joseph story as the subject of the formula in 37:1. Moreover, *two* specifications of place follow, each controlled by the preposition *bet*, each constructed with the noun *'ereṣ* and a closer definition of the place: *bᵉ'ereṣ miṣrayim bᵉereṣ gōšen.* "Israel dwelt in the land of Egypt, in the land of Goshen."

Thus, it appears to me that the opening sentence of the Joseph story has been constructed, not only on the basis of a common narrative formula, also present in 36:8, but also on the basis of an exact parallel with the closing sentence of the Joseph story. The parallel suggests, moreover, *a structural dialectic in the Joseph story itself.* The scope of the story, according to the opening and closing sentences, ranges from Jacob in Canaan to Israel in Egypt. It is clear that symmetry of structure is characteristic for the entire Joseph story. If the structure of the story is to be understood adequately, this example of symmetry must not be overlooked.

The personal names of the patriarch in the two sentences, it might be objected, argue against such a tight symmetrical unity between 37:1 and 47:27a. A more extensive evaluation of names as criteria for making source distinctions in the Joseph story will be set out below, in chapter II. For now it is sufficient to note that in the Joseph story the names Jacob and Israel interchange without suggesting composite contexts. One could compare, for example, Gen 37 (vss. 13 and 34), 42 (vss. 5 and 1,4,29,36), 45 (vss. 21,28 and 25,27), 46 (vss. 1-2,5,8,29,30 and 2,5-6,8,18-19,22,25-27), and finally 47 (vss. 27 and 7-10). Only Gen 43 carries the name Israel without mixing in the name Jacob (cf. vss. 6,8,11). The names are significant. But they do not necessarily signify disunity, much less an inferior narrative source.[5] To the contrary, they point to a basic shift in perspective from the tribal orientation of the patriarchal traditions to the people orientation of the exodus traditions (cf. especially 47:27b). Jacob in Canaan. Israel in Egypt.

This hypothesis leaves the *toledoth* formula unexplained. It may well be that the formula enters the exposition of the Joseph story on the basis of an

[5] Against Redford, pp. 26, 131–135.

analogy with 36:8–9.[6] But even so, it functions in its present position in a fashion that does not disrupt the unity of the exposition. Secondary or not, it marks the beginning of the exposition's presentation of major characters and their relationships. Redford argues to the contrary that the *toledoth* formula can introduce genealogies, as it does, for example, in Gen 5:1 (although there vss. 2–4 intervene between the formula and the genealogy). This observation leads him to suggest that the *toledoth* formula in 37:2 originally came before the name list in Gen 46:8–27.[7] He then assumes that the two originally united elements were broken apart in order to insert the Joseph story because chronologically the Joseph story must have preceded Jacob's move to Egypt. One could object that in that case the Joseph story would not be inserted between the formula and the list, but split apart by the list, since the conclusion of the story comes in 46:28–47:27. But the hypothesis fails for a different reason: The list in Gen 46:8 is not properly a genealogy. It is similar, to be sure. It follows an order of names also present in genealogies (cf. Gen 35:22b–26). It shows contact with a genealogy especially in vss. 15,18,22,25. But the list, perhaps derived originally from a genealogy, has a distinct function. It now serves as an organizational scheme, a register for the people who went to Egypt with Jacob. With this function, the list has more in common with the lists in Ex 1:1–5; Num 1:5–16,20–46; 13:4–16; 26:5–51. Moreover, the list in Gen 46:8–27 already has an introduction, commensurate with its function: "These are the names of the sons of Israel who came to Egypt, Jacob and his sons." (Cf. the introductions to the lists in Ex 1:1–5; Num 1:5–16, 20–46: 13:4–16; 26:5–51). And it concludes, like Num 1:20–46 and 26: 5–51, with the number of people encompassed by the list. Thus, with its change in function, the list in Gen 46:8–27 no longer qualifies as a genealogy.[8] This argument would not justify denying a *toledoth* formula as the introduction to the list if it were already there (thus, cf. Num 1:20). It is intended to deny conclusions that reconstruct a distant name list now equipped with a different kind of introduction as the original continuation of 37:2.

The *toledoth* formula can function in conjunction with statements like the one in 47:28 (cf. Gen 6:9–10 and 9:28–29).[9] The purpose of the combination would be to frame the outer limits of a narrative. I have suggested elsewhere (cf. note 3) that Gen 47:28 introduces the framework narrative about Jacob's

---

[6]So, Redford, p. 14. On the other hand, Noth, p. 18, n. 53, observes: "The introduction in 37:2 is probably only an imitation of the Toledoth-book formula and does not prove that the following comes from the Toledoth-book."

[7]Redford, pp. 3–14.

[8]Redford, p. 9, makes the function of administrative lists quite clear. Moreover, he implies a distinction between administrative lists used to control tax-payers and draftees and genealogies used to support positions of families in power during shifting social structures.

[9]Sean E. McEvenue, *The Narrative Style of the Priestly Writer* (*An Bib* 50; Rome: Pontifical Biblical Institute, 1971) 36–41.

death. This point holds, particularly when 47:28 is compared with the introduction to the unit presenting Joseph's death, Gen 50:22. This observation, however, does not vitiate a conclusion that the *toledoth* formula plus the entire narrative about Jacob's death constitutes a frame for the Joseph story. The Joseph story would in fact reveal two frames. Gen 37:1 and its parallel in 47:27a set the principal frame for the story, while Gen 37:2, the *toledoth* formula; interjects the story into a larger context of traditions about Jacob.

Following the *toledoth* formula a nominal sentence introduces Joseph by specifying his age, his occupation, and his relationship with his brothers.[10] Significantly, the brothers are not introduced one by one with corresponding data, but as a group. Moreover, they are subordinated to Joseph by being defined simply as Joseph's brothers. "Joseph, seventeen years old, was a shepherd with his brothers among the sheep." Even the following division of the brothers according to their mothers does not soften the subordination since the mothers are defined as wives *of Joseph's father*. Vs. 2b contains the first element of narration in the story: "Joseph brought a bad tale about them to their father." Yet, it too must be seen as a part of the exposition, since it sets the principal crisis for the plot of the entire story, a destructive tension between Joseph and his brothers.

It is possible to deny that vs. 2 following the *toledoth* formula has any functional unity with the primary stage of the Joseph story exposition.[11] The reasons are: 1) The references to Joseph's age and the names of the brothers' mothers are not characteristic for the major narration style exhibited in most parts of the Joseph story. 2) The note about Joseph's occupation as a shepherd contradicts his privileged position in the remaining parts of the chapter. 3) Vs. 2 gives a reason for the brothers' hatred markedly different from the rest of the chapter. 4) The verse apparently has the complete Joseph story in view. Source critics have long noted these problems and used them to distinguish parallel lines of the exposition. And perhaps these points do suggest that the verse is not closely united with vss. 3–4. Conclusions must remain tentative.

Yet, vs. 2 appears to function well with the following verses of the exposition. The following points should be noted: 1) The data about Joseph and the brothers have parallels in 41:46–47 and perhaps in 41:50–52. These data are not the kinds of information that constitute grist for a narrative, but rather they provide the substance for interludes or expositions. 2) Joseph's

---

[10]For a discussion of grammar and syntax in expositions, cf. W. Richter, *Die sogenannten vorprophetischen Berufungs-berichte. Eine literaturwissenschaftliche Studie zu 1 Sam 9,1–10,16, Ex 3f. und Ri 6,11b–17.* (*FRLANT* 101; Göttingen: Vandenhoeck und Ruprecht, 1970) 30–31, as well as the literature noted there.

[11]Cf. Claus Westermann, "Die Joseph-Erzählung," in *Calwer Predigthilfen* 5 (Stuttgart: Calwer, 1970) 30. Redford, pp. 14–16

occupation as shepherd is noted in a general introduction to the story, not in the development of the narrative. But in any case, could Joseph not be a shepherd, like his brothers, and receive favored treatment by exemption from work? He stays at home, not because he is not a shepherd, but because his father pampers him. And the pampering adds to the tension of the narrative. 3) The reason for the brothers' hatred is different in vs. 2 from the ones noted in the following verses. But a different reason for a crucial element does not constitute evidence for denying the unity of the verse with its context. Rather, it is a part of a structural device, reflecting the symmetry of the exposition: Vs. 2 introduces Joseph, a privileged son among his brothers, and notes his contribution to the crisis relationship. Vs. 3 introduces the father with specification of his contribution to the crisis. Again in nominal sentence order, the verse notes Israel's love for Joseph more than for all the other brothers. This notation may not be an explicit contribution to the crisis relationship. A father can love one son more than others without alienating the family. But the crisis is nevertheless implicit. It emphasizes Joseph's pampered position. And the implicit crisis is made explicit in vs. 3b. The father gives Joseph a special robe, a visible sign of his exalted position.[12] The entire verse thus heightens the crisis between Joseph and his brothers. And vs. 4 adds the brothers' response: "They hated him, and they were not able to speak to him in peace."

The exposition thus stands together as a well constructed unit. And its function as exposition presupposes that it has the complete Joseph story in view. By its symmetry it presents the principal figures for the entire plot and shows the distinctive contribution of each to the tension that holds the plot together. No single figure is responsible for the alienation of the family. To the contrary, all share the burden of the broken relationships.

II. COMPLICATION (37:5–36)

The second structural element in the Joseph story contains three principal parts: A. a group of two dream reports (vss. 5–11); B. a narration of events leading to the principal crisis of the narrative (vss. 12–33); and C. a concluding soliloquy (vss. 34–35). The dream reports might as easily be considered a part of the exposition, particularly since they have a foreshadowing function in the structure of the Joseph story as a whole (cf. the discussion below).[13] To draw the distinction too rigidly would violate the interaction of the narrative. Yet, the dreams play an explicit role in the complication, a foundation for the brothers' radical action in the following

---

[12] So, Westermann, pp. 30–34.
[13] So, von Rad, *Genesis,* p. 352. Westermann, p. 29, takes all of ch. 37 as exposition. But cf. the parallel construction between the complication, 37:5–36, and the second stage of complication, ch. 42.

verses. For that reason, the dreams are taken here as a part of the complication element.

Vs. 36 can properly represent D., a fourth structural element in the scene. It is nonetheless not a principal part of the scene but rather a secondary transition to the third scene.

A. The two dream reports, vss. 5–8 and 9–11, are constructed in parallel with each other; again, the symmetry of construction so characteristic for the Joseph story comes clearly to the surface.[14] In vs. 5 a general introduction to the first dream makes prominent use of the vocable, ḥlm, "dream" both as verb (wayyaḥălōm) and as noun. "Joseph dreamed a dream." This introduction should be understood as a narration element in third person, stamped by a first person call to attention in a speech reporting a dream. The point of the observation is that insofar as I can see the weight of the eivdence, the first person dream report speech constitutes the primary context for stereotyping the structure of dream reports generally, with third person narrative reports drawn from such speeches (cf. the comments on dream report speeches, particularly the call to attention, below). Vs. 5 then notes that Joseph narrated his dream to his brothers, with the brothers' response picking up the key term from vs. 4 in the exposition: "He told it to his brothers, and they *hated* him all the more." Vss. 6–7 detail the dream speech. With the catchword, dream, again prominent (hahălôm hazzeh 'ăšer hālāmtî), vs. 6 summons the brothers to attention. The function of this element as a call to attention is clarified by the 2.m.pl. Qal imperative from the verb šmʿ: "Hear now. . . ." That imperative is then coupled with words from the characteristic root hlm (cf. Gen 40:8,9; 41:15; Jgs 7:13; Jer 23:25; Dan 2:3). And vs. 7, the core of the dream report, narrates the progress of the dream under the initial stamp of the particle hinnēh, "behold." Vs. 8 then reports the brothers' reaction with a pair of rhetorical questions and a concluding comment: "'Will you indeed have dominion over us?' So they *hated* him again because of his dreams [pl.] and his words." Thus, the principal crisis intensifies. But the dream also anticipates the brothers' subjugation to Joseph's power and foreshadows the account in Gen 42 that brings the brothers in humble submission to an "unknown" but powerful administrator in the court of Egypt.

Vs. 9a introduces the second dream with a general statement parallel to vs. 5 (wayyaḥălōm 'ôd hălôm 'aḥēr). "He dreamed another dream." The continuation of the introduction notes only that Joseph reported the dream to his brothers; no reference to the brothers' response appears. Vs. 9b then details Joseph's description of his dream in a speech constructed in the same

---

[14]Structural characteristics of dream reports have been described in detail by W. Richter, "Traum und Traumdeutung im AT," *BZ* 7 (1963) 202–220, and earlier by E. L. Ehrlich, *Der Traum im Alten Testament* (*BZAW* 73; Berlin: Töpelmann, 1953) 1–45 and 58–85. My analysis of structure in the dream reports of the Joseph story builds on that foundation.

pattern, although not in as much detail as vss. 6–7. Vs. 9b would be a call to attention, with the vocable *ḥlm* the central feature: *hinnēh ḥālamtî ḥălôm 'ôd*. "Behold I dreamed another dream." This element is not so obviously a call to attention as the one in vs. 6. It has no imperative from the verb *šm'*. But the parallel construction with vs.6 makes it clear that this briefer formula serves the same function. Vs. 9bb then narrates the dream, introduced with the particle *hinnēh*. This dream also describes the brothers' humble submission to Joseph. But it adds a distinctive element: Joseph's father and mother as well as his brothers will eventually bow before their dreamer. This dream foreshadows Gen 43 through 47:27, the account of the brothers' second trip to Egypt, Joseph's self-revelation, and the final entry of Jacob and his people into Goshen. Significantly, the objection Jacob raises against the second dream, vs. 10, emphasizes his coming (*hăbô' nābô'*) to Joseph. The same verb appears again in the scene of Jacob's arrival in Goshen (cf. Gen 46:31; 47:1–5). Vss. 10–11 then detail the response of both the father, again in two rhetorical questions (vs. 10), and the brothers (vs. 11). And again, the response emphasizes the brothers' tense relationship with Joseph, contrasted in this case with the father's anticipation for Joseph's future.

Two problems in the development of these dream reports demand somewhat greater detail in this analysis. 1) The second dream suggests that both father and mother will bow before their son. But the mother of Joseph plays no further role in the structure of the dream report and indeed no other role at all in the Joseph story. To the contrary, the general assumption in the story seems to be that the mother of Joseph was dead. If the dream does indeed foreshadow the concluding elements in the plot of the Joseph story, then one may conclude that the allusion to the mother in vs. 10 need not suggest that Rachel was still alive and that, as a consequence, this dream breaks the unity of the context. To the contrary, it simply facilitates the sun—moon motif at the center of the dream as a symbol of the family. The reference to the mother, in that case, would appear only because of the astral imagery of the dream.[15]

2) Wolfgang Richter proposes a detailed structure for dream reports, including "1. Anzeige des Traumes 2. Traumeröffnungsformel 3. Traumkorpus 4. Deutung 5. Erfüllung."[16] It seems to me, however, that one must not insist too rigidly on the completion of the structure. Richter's observation is accurate that the dreams in ch. 37 have no immediate notice of fulfillment but rather anticipate fulfillment in the total scope of the story. He is correct also in placing such a structure as an original part of a literary construct. But

---

[15] Against H. Gressmann, "Ursprung und Entwicklung der Joseph-Sage," in EYXAPICTH-PION. *Studien zur Religion und Literatur des Alten und Neuen Testaments.* (*FRLANT* 36, Göttingen: Vandenhoeck und Ruprecht, 1923) 18–19. Arguments for mythological elements in the Joseph story based on this dream report also seem poorly founded. Cf. von Rad, *Genesis,* p. 351–352.

[16] Richter, "Traum," p. 204.

can one conclude that any dream report missing a fulfillment notice reflects either such literary construction or an incomplete pattern? Moreover, is the interpretation a necessary element of a dream report genre? Or is it a distinct element in the narration? Does the narrator not use dream report elements and interpretation elements at his own discretion in order to construct his material according to his own design? Can we not understand the role of the dream reports more adequately if we define the interpretation and the fulfillment as collateral elements in the larger narration rather than as necessary elements in dream reports? Such a position would, incidentally, avoid an apparent necessity for defining two distinct dream report structures, one with an interpretation of the dream and one so obvious as to need no interpretation.

Thus, the dreams intensify the crisis of the story. The brothers hate Joseph the more. And that hate gains explicit expression in the second part of the scene. But the dreams also define the scope of the story. The principal crisis is a break in the family. That crisis will not be resolved until the entire family, not only the brothers, but also the father with his people, come to Joseph in recognition of his power.[17] Insofar as the dreams are concerned, then, Jacob's move with his family from Canaan to Egypt is a crucial part of the story's scope. Jacob in Canaan. Israel in Egypt.

B. The tense relationships between the brothers and Joseph rise to a peak in vss. 12–33, the second part of the scene. Following a brief introduction in. vs. 12, vss. 13–14a move Joseph away from the protection of his father and into the control of his brothers. In the formal structure of a conversation, Jacob commissions Joseph, who is exempt from the responsibilities of shepherding, to investigate the well-being of his brothers. The word šālôm in vs. 14 echoes the use of the same word in vs. 4 with ironic force. The brother who could provoke no word of šālôm from his brothers must now check on his brothers' šālôm. Then vs. 14b changes the setting from Jacob's home and protection to Shechem.[18]

But Joseph's stop in Shechem does not produce the results anticipated by the commission. He finds no trace of his brothers. Rather, an unnamed man of Shechem finds Joseph wandering in a field, asks about his search, and provides the information about the brothers necessary for continuing the

---

[17] The reference to Joseph's "kingship" in the brothers' reaction to the dreams should not be taken as an allusion to the future kingship in Israel. But neither should it support a reconstruction of the story to picture Joseph as king in Egypt. It functions only to emphasize the brothers' strong reaction to Joseph. Against Gunkel, *Genesis*, p. 405. H. Gunkel, "Die Komposition der Josephsgeschichte," *ZDMG* 77 (1922) 69; Gressmann, p. 20. So, von Rad, *Genesis*, p. 352.

[18] Structural movement within this scene, as well as in other major structural elements of the Joseph story, is commonly indicated by a change in physical location. This observation highlights one of my major contentions, namely, that structure in the Joseph story as a whole builds on the crucial change in physical location from Canaan to Egypt.

narration. The interlude in vss. 15–17a, constructed as a conversation between Joseph and his unnamed benefactor, does not advance the story. Indeed, the unnamed man drops out of sight as quickly as he appeared. But these points should not suggest that the interlude is secondary or an interpolation that breaks the unity of these verses with the context. The interlude functions simply as a delay in the pace of action, a stylistic retardation to build anticipation for Joseph's confrontation with his brothers. Vs. 17b then completes the change of setting. Joseph finds his brothers in Dothan.

With vs. 18 the narration shifts from Joseph to his brothers. A dialogue among the brothers, vss. 18–22, shows a plot to dispose of Joseph developing just as Joseph approaches in the distance. The opening speech (vss. 19–20) identifies the object of the plot as the dreamer (*ba'al hahălōmôt hallāzeh*) and thus ties the narration directly to the dreams in vss. 5–11. The dreams obviously have struck sensitive points. The remaining part of the speech employs a 1.pl. cohortative following an imperative and must be seen as a type of self-admonition among the brothers to execute a plan. Reuben's first speech, vs. 21, follows the same pattern, cast as a 1.pl. cohortative appeal for an alternative plan. The second speech, vs. 22, breaks the self-admonition pattern, however, and sets out details for an alternative plan as if Reuben initially refused participation in the plans to kill the brother. (For comments on this doubling of Reuben's speech as characteristic style, cf. below, Ch. II.) The verb here is a 2.m.pl. Qal imperfect with *'al* negation. In both cases (vss. 21ab and 22b) the text explains the purpose for Reuben's suggestion. Confining Joseph in a pit might be construed as a plan to kill Joseph by starvation. If that were the case, the other brothers might be expected to accept the alternative as a way around direct physical attack. That impression would have strengthened Judah's continuing concern about killing Joseph (vs. 26).[19] But the continuing narration makes it quite clear that Reuben intended Joseph no harm. He intended instead to rescue Joseph from the murder and return him to his father.

Some degree of disunity makes a clear understanding of progression in the narrative from this point difficult. A new dialogue among the brothers in vss. 25–27a alters Reuben's plan to prevent Joseph's death: Judah recommends that, rather than killing Joseph, the brothers might well profit by selling him to passing merchants (cf. vs. 26: *mah-beṣa'*). That plan is executed. And as a consequence, Joseph's fate for the coming days, the subject of the remaining parts of the story, falls into the hands of strangers on their way *to Egypt.*

---

[19] Rainer Kessler, *Die Querverweise im Pentateuch. Überlieferungsgeschichtliche Untersuchung der expliziten Querverbindungen innerhalb des vorpriesterlichen Pentateuchs* (unpublished dissertation, Heidelberg, 1972) 147.

Two problems confront the interpretation of this section. 1) How does one evaluate a second plan to save Joseph from death? There is no apparent reason that I can see that demands interpretation of this evidence as disruptive in the progress of the narration. It presupposes confinement in the pit, a part of Reuben's plan. The confinement would apparently cast the image of exposure and starvation as a means for executing the brother without spilling his blood in violent attack. It would also presuppose that Reuben was not present during the process of revising his plan. Reuben's cry of lament in vs. 29 also suggests that he knew nothing of the new plan. That two different plans to save Joseph appear seems to me to offer no great problem in the unity of the narration. There is a difference in the two plans. But the difference emphasizes Reuben's isolation from the other brothers. And it suggests that while Judah's plan may save Joseph from death, it exposes him to a fate that could be as bad.

2) The new plan calls initially for selling Joseph to Ishmaelite traders. But then a group of Midianites passes by, draws Joseph from the pit, and finally delivers him to his destination with the Ishmaelites for a price of twenty pieces of silver. The sudden appearance of the Midianites breaks the flow of the narrative and points to an element of disunity in the section. If, however, the reference to the Midianites in vs. 28 could be taken as a gloss, a secondary intrusion into the text, the problem would be clarified.[20] In that case the brothers would be the subject of the plural verbs following the reference to the Midianites. Moreover, various allusions to the event would support the hypothesis that the brothers were primarily responsible for disposing of Joseph. In vs. 27 the brothers deliberate about *selling* Joseph. In 42:22 the brothers confess their guilt, their sin against the boy. And in 45:4-5 Joseph observes that the brothers sold him into an Egyptian slavery. The allusion to the event in 40:15 is more problematic. Joseph states that "I was stolen from the land of the Hebrews." But that description need not imply the Midianite action. It has only the brothers' act in view, although it uses the verb *gnb* rather than *mkr*. The hypothesis can be supported by reference to Ex 21:16 and Dt 24:7 where the verbs *gnb* and *mkr* are set side by side. *Mkr* is the verb from Gen 37:27 and 45:4-5, *gnb* the parallel verb for the same event in 40:15.

To treat the reference to the Midianites in vs. 28 as a gloss would nevertheless require some reasonable suggestion that a problem lay in the text and motivated the explanation. The purpose of the change might be to alleviate the problem posed by brothers selling one of their own into slavery, a crime of major proportions punishable by death (cf. Ex 21:16; Dt 24:7). It would seem to me to be reasonable, therefore, to suggest that the reference to the Midianites in vs. 28 is a secondary intrusion into the text, not an original part of the Joseph story tradition. (On 37:36 and 39:1, cf. below.)

[20] Cf. Kessler, p. 149-150.

Finally, vss. 31–32a change the setting again. The brothers prepare an alibi for Joseph's loss, ironically with the robe of superiority, and return to the father. The dialogue between the sons and father, vss. 32ab–33, calls first for legal recognition of the prepared evidence and concludes when the father affirms the loss of his son.[21] The crisis of the Joseph story is thus clear: The family is broken apart. The break comes to its peak in the brothers' treachery. But it is perpetuated by the brothers' careful plan to deceive the father. If the brothers are to continue in Jacob's family, at least until the reconciliation, they must do so by maintaining deception as a way of life.

C. The chapter then sets out Jacob's mourning, including a lamentation soliloquy (cf. 2 Sam 18:33). The father considers Joseph dead. The brothers can do nothing to alter their plan. Vss. 34–35 capture the desperate character of the crisis by narrating Jacob's mourning for his dead favorite son. And the soliloquy in vs. 35 emphasizes the point: "I shall go down to Sheol to my son, mourning."

Yet, the tension between the brothers and Joseph has not been resolved. It has only been postponed. Joseph is not dead. He has been sold into Egypt. Moreover, when Jacob laments that reunion is possible only by his own descent, does the narrative not anticipate Jacob's descent to Joseph in Egypt? Not only does the speech note explicitly that Jacob's descent will be to Joseph, but the verb controlling the statement, a 1.s. Qal imperfect from *yrd*, has a significant parallel in 45:9, a description of Jacob's descent to Joseph in Egypt. 45:13 parallels this point appropriately with a Hiph'il form of the same verb. 46:3–4 offer a more exact point of comparison, although these verses appear in secondary material (cf. also 42:2,3,38; 43:4,5, 11,15,20,22; 44:21,23,26, all pointing to the brothers, either the ten or Benjamin, who must go down to Egypt). The only other principal use of the verb in the Joseph story describes movement to Sheol in the event of Jacob's death (cf. 42:38; 44:29,31). Moreover, the crucial verb here would contrast with the exodus verb *'lh* (cf. 45:9; 46:4). The opposite of Jacob's despair over the loss of Joseph (despair over leaving Canaan for Egypt?) would be his joy over discovery that Joseph is alive (joy over the exodus?). This parallel must be followed with caution. The joy of the father comes only in finding that Joseph is alive. At least it is clear, however, that the structural dialectic, Canaan-Egypt, functions in the scene. Joseph has gone. Jacob must follow.

D. Vs. 36 emphasizes the move through notation that Joseph was sold to an Egyptian, Potiphar. But the verse is not developed. Rather, the subjects, Potiphar and his purchase, drop from view in the face of a totally new topic in ch. 38. The verse thus appears to be an anticlimax to the scene, isolated from the major movement of the scene's narration.

The complication in the structure of the story thus details the principal

---

[21] David Daube, "Law in the Narratives," in *Studies in Biblical Law* (New York: KTAV, 1969) 3–10.

crisis in the story's plot. But it also anticipates the denouement of the story. Joseph's family is torn apart. The rift appears to be as permanent as death. But it will finally be reconciled. At the same time, the scene points to an internal unity with the next elements of structure. Joseph is in the hands of a caravan, going to Egypt. He will rise to power there, using his power to subjugate his hapless brothers. The scene demonstrates, moreover, that the move from Canaan to Egypt is *the* principal structural focus in the story's plot. It is not a move involving simply a quest for food in the face of famine. It is a fundamental relocation of principal figures. Joseph moves there, not because he seeks food or fortune, but because he is no longer free to choose his own course. Jacob will move there because he wants to rejoin his son. And that move will constitute the denouement of the plot, the final reconciliation of the family.[22]

One additional observation may now be in order. From the beginning of the story, Joseph is the typical spoiled child, favored by his father, hated by his brothers. And he does nothing to improve his relationship with his family. He reports his dreams to his brothers, almost as if in condescension to taunt them with his superiority. And his brothers hate him for it. Von Rad notes this audacious behavior. He suggests, however, that if a dream were to have prophetic significance in the ancient world, it must be spoken, reported to the proper sources.[23] This may well be true. But the dreams contribute to the tension. In the structure of the scene, they constitute the principal drive in compounding bad relationships between Joseph and his brothers. Thus, in vss. 18–20, the brothers conspire against the "lord of the dreams" when they see him approaching in the distance. Von Rad argues that the expression, *ba'al hahălōmôt*, means one empowered to receive prophetic dreams. This again may well be true. But the context of the expression must render it in this case as sarcastic. I do not intend to deny the dark and irrevocable character of prophetic dreams that von Rad describes. I intend only to emphasize that the structure of the scene uses Joseph's dreams to highlight the point of hostility between Joseph and the brothers. And in that context, recitation of the dreams cannot be excused lightly. It has a marked negative quality.

III.   DIGRESSION (39–41)

The next element of structure is more complex than the first two, yet it shows a remarkable symmetry and artistic skill in conception. Its three

[22]Hannelis Schulte, *Die Entstehung der Geschichtsschreibung im Alten Israel* (*BZAW* 128; Berlin: Töpelmann, 1972) 24–27, suggests that an earlier stage in the history of the story narrated only an account of descent into Egypt in order to seek food. Cf. the evaluation below, in ch. II.

[23]Von Rad, *Genesis*, p. 352–355.

principal scenes constitute a subplot for the Joseph story, a digression from
the movement of the principal plot established in ch. 37.

A. The first scene in the digression, Gen 39:1–20a, develops a clear
pattern of its own: Joseph faces a crisis, rises above it to a position of power,
and executes the position with finesse. The scene opens with Joseph sold into
slavery, a foreigner subjected to an Egyptian master. The first element of the
scene (vss. 1–6) is an exposition for the coming narration, introduced with
nominal sentence construction. No biographical data for Joseph appear in
vs. 1. But Potiphar is presented in full detail: "Potiphar, an officer of the
Pharaoh, the captain of the guard, an Egyptian. . . ." And the master-slave
relationship between Potiphar and Joseph is defined. Since this sentence
functions as an introduction for a principal character in the scene, its
· primary role in the Joseph story must be seen here, not in the parallel
sentence in 37:36. To be sure, the name Potiphar does not appear again in
the chapter. But the narration refers to Joseph's master as "the Egyptian"
(cf. vs. 2). And 39:1 notes explicitly that Potiphar is "the Egyptian."
Moreover, the verse functions intrinsically in the structure of ch. 39 since it
plays a fundamental role in the introduction of the scene. But the verse in
37:36 stands isolated from the major movement of structure in its immediate
context. The 37:36 parallel would thus be properly understood as a secondary imitation of 39:1, used for incorporating the narrative in Gen 38 into the
framework of the Joseph story.[24] And significantly 37:36, a secondary
imitation, carries the only reference to the Midianites in the Joseph story
other than 37:28 (cf. the discussion of the Midianites above).

Vs. 2a*a* in Gen 39 offsets Joseph's subordination to Potiphar with a
formula expressing Yahweh's assistance: *way⁽e⁾hî 'ǎdōnāy 'et-yôsēp.*[25] As a
result of the divine assistance, not to mention Joseph's own skill, Joseph's
work prospers, and he receives full charge of the household as vss. 3–4 show
clearly: "His master saw that Yahweh was with him, and that Yahweh
caused all that he did to prosper in his hands. So Joseph found favor in his
[Potiphar's] eyes. He [Joseph] served him [*way⁽e⁾šāret 'ōtô*], and he [Potiphar]
appointed him [*wayyapqîdēhû*] over all his house. And all that he had he
gave into his hand." Vss. 5–6a correspond with the emphasis of this formula.
This part of the first scene, however, does not belong to the primary
narration of the element. Although it is presented as a series of events in the
past, it nevertheless defines the relationship between Joseph and his master
and must be considered a part of the scene's opening exposition. This
conclusion is confirmed by a single item of biographical information for
Joseph in vs. 6b: "Joseph was handsome in form and good-looking." The

[24] Contrary to Speiser, *Genesis,* pp. 302–304; Gunkel, *Genesis,* p. 423.

[25] Westermann, p. 47, comments about contact with patriarchal traditions in this verse. Cf.
more recently, N. Habel, *Literary Criticism of the Old Testament* (Philadelphia: Fortress, 1971)
59–60.

obvious purpose for the exposition as a whole, and particularly vs. 6b, is to set the stage for the major body of the scene in vss. 7–20a. Since Joseph was handsome, Potiphar's wife was interested.

The complication that gives character to the major body of the scene is, of course, the invitation offered Joseph by his master's wife (cf. vss. 7–20a). The formula in vs. 7aa, *way*ᵉ*hî 'ahar hadd*ᵉ*bārîm hā'ēlleh,* does not mark a major transition to a new scene, but a movement from the exposition to the specific crisis within a single scene (cf. Gen 40:1). Vss. 7abb–9 then develop the crucial conversation between Potiphar's wife and Joseph. Potiphar's wife invites, in effect, instructs Joseph to sleep with her, and Joseph refuses to execute the instructions. Joseph's rejection in vss. 8–9 describes compliance with the woman's invitation, should it have been given, as a sin against God. But the structure of the response makes the trust of responsibility the master laid on Joseph's shoulders the explicit reason for Joseph's reaction. The appeal to a sin against God is only a description of the act he rejects. "With me, my master does not know what is in the house. All which he has he has given into my hand. There is no one in this house greater than I. He has withheld nothing from me except you, because you are his wife. How shall I do this great evil thing and sin against God?" The response does not argue: "Because this thing is a sin against God, I shall not do it." It argues: "Because this thing violates the charge of my master to oversee all in his house, I shall not do this sin against God." At the height of the scene, then, the focus of interest falls on Joseph's responsible administration of his office.[26]

Vss. 10–20a develop the crisis of the scene with a narration of the woman's plot to trap Joseph. The crisis thus does not lie in the possibility that Joseph might accept the woman's invitation, but in what the woman might do when Joseph refuses. Moreover, the crisis does not appear in narration of events. To the contrary, two speeches by the woman, one to Joseph (vs. 12a) and one to the servants she calls to witness her evidence against Joseph (vss. 14b–15), carry the weight of the narrative. With the evidence left behind in Joseph's final flight from the woman's lair, the woman accuses Joseph of initiating the contact. And the accusation is obviously false (cf. vss. 14b–15). The penalty for such an accusation, if it were substantiated, would be death. Thus, as in ch. 37, so here Joseph faces a life and death crisis. Vss. 16–20a, however, do not bring Joseph to a point of death. The woman repeats her false accusation to her husband (vss. 17b–18), and the husband has Joseph confined in prison. But whether he faces a death sentence the scene does not say. To the contrary, the scene stops in mid-stream, leaving its audience in full suspense. The symmetry of the scene cannot be denied. The woman repeats her invitation, then she repeats her accusation. And the symmetry serves the artistry of the plot. Joseph moves now fast, now almost painfully

---

[26] George W. Coats, "The Joseph Story and Ancient Wisdom: A Reappraisal," *CBQ* 35 (1973) 285–297.

slowly toward a fate that would bring the story as a whole to an untimely end. But the scene does not specify the outcome of the crisis one way or the other. To the contrary, the crisis leading to Joseph's confinement in prison provides *only* a vision of Joseph's stoic stature as an administrator falsely accused of foolish behavior, yet faithful to his responsibility to the end. And in the process, it sets the stage for the second scene. Any possible disposition of charges against Joseph bears no crucial importance for the narration.

B. The second scene in the digression develops in precisely the same pattern as the first. It begins in vs. 20b with Joseph again at the mercy of a master, this time the captain of the prison. The opening exposition is much shorter here than in the first scene, yet the same pattern of structure and the same function can easily be recognized. Vs. 20b defines the disposition Joseph faces in the scene (cf. 39:1b). Vs. 21a follows with the formula for Yahweh's assistance (cf. 39:2a). The second figure of the scene, the captain of the prison, is introduced briefly in vs. 21b. Even though he has not appeared previously in the Joseph story, he merits no biographical data, and indeed, no name. And his introduction is combined with a definition of his relationship with Joseph: "He [Yahweh] gave him [Joseph] favor in the eyes of the captain of the prison" (cf. 39:4). Vss. 22–23 then present Joseph's elevation to a position of authority over the other prisoners with a note about the successful consequences of his work. The formulation of this segment in the exposition follows closely the parallel segment in the first scene, 39:4–6a, and thus contributes to the basic symmetry of the story's design. Thus: "The captain of the prison gave all the prisoners who were in the prison into Joseph's hand. And all which was done there, he was the doer. The captain of the prison did not see [what was] in his hand, for Yahweh was with him. And whatever he did, Yahweh made prosperous."

The formula in 40:1aα marks the transition from exposition to the major body of the scene, just as it did in 39:7. The development of the crisis in the major body, however, breaks the parallel somewhat. Vs. 1aβb introduces two new characters simply with a definition of their relationship with the Pharaoh: "The cup-bearer of the king of Egypt and the baker sinned against their master, the king of Egypt." Vss. 2–3 then bring the two servants of the Pharaoh into contact with Joseph. And vs. 4 defines the relationship: "The captain of the prison appointed Joseph with them." These verses might thus be considered a part of the exposition.[27] This possibility seems stronger since the captain of the guard, an unnamed figure introduced in 39:21, plays no major role in the body of the scene, but rather provides the occasion to bring Joseph and the Pharaoh's servants together. Moreover, the crucial event that constitutes the substance in the major body of the scene comes to light

---

[27] So, L. Ruppert, *Die Josepherzählung der Genesis. Ein Beitrag zur Theologie der Penta-teuchquellen.* (*StANT* 11; München: Kösel, 1965) 61–62. Gunkel, *Genesis,* p. 428.

only in vss. 5ff. And it is distinguished from the introduction of the Pharaoh's servants by a transition formula in vs. 4b. But the plot of the major body in the scene depends on the notation about relationship between the two new characters and the Pharaoh in vss. 1–2. The cup-bearer and the baker offended the Pharaoh. Their dreams foreshadow the Pharaoh's disposition of their offenses. Although the structure of the scene appears somewhat more loosely formed here than in the first scene, particularly in vss. 1abb–4, all of vss. 1–23 should be considered the major body of narration. The formula in vs. 1aa would confirm this conclusion.

Von Rad observes that even though the parallel between the expositions in the two scenes is exact, the major development of plot in the second diverges rather sharply from the first.[28] This observation is correct. But the direction of its impact must be more carefully controlled than von Rad's suggestions allow. He argues that in the second scene Joseph is apparently made a servant for the two new prisoners. In a servant's role, he could not occupy an office of power among the prisoners, parallel to the office of power he holds in the temptress scene. The text in question is 40:4: "The captain of the guard appointed Joseph with them [wayyipqōd . . . 'et-yōsēp 'ittām] and he served them [wayᵉšāret 'ōtām]." The key for interpreting this text lies in understanding the two verbs, "to appoint" (pqd) and "to serve," (šrt). Both appear in the parallel scene, in 39:4. The verb pqd means "to place in a position of authority, a position of power." (Cf. Num 3:10; 4:27; Jer 15:3; 49:19; 51:27; et al.). Thus, in 39:4, Joseph was given a position of power over Potiphar's household. But the prepositions normally used with this construction are 'al (39:4) or 'el. In 40:4 the preposition is 'et. The verb šrt, "to serve," appears in the parallel scene in 39:4, where Joseph serves, not the household whom he has authority over, but his master, Potiphar (cf. the collocation wayᵉšāret 'ōtô). This parallel provides a clue for understanding 40:4. Joseph has been given authority over the prisoners; the captain of the guard put them all "in his hand," just as Potiphar put his household into Joseph's hand. That position of responsibility he maintains. When the two servants of the Pharaoh enter the scene, however, the source of Joseph's authority shifts. He now serves, not the captain of the guard, but the cup-bearer and the baker. But his position is not menial slave. His position is one of responsibility, analogous to his relationships with Potiphar in the previous scene. In effect, the cup-bearer and the baker replace the captain of the guard as principals in the scene. And significantly, the captain of the guard does not appear again after the two new characters are introduced. Moreover, the collocation wayyipqōd . . . 'et-yōsēp 'ittām, fits into the picture of a shift in authority lines. Joseph was appointed over the household, and in the appointment he served Potiphar. He was appointed over the

[28] Von Rad, Genesis, pp. 369–370.

prison, but in relationship with the servants of the Pharaoh. And he served them in the same manner that he served Potiphar.

The shift in authority and, indeed, the shift in structural symmetry from the pattern of the first scene underline the distinct structural focus of the second scene. Here the concern of the narration is not with the administration of Joseph's office over the other prisoners but with an interpretation of his masters' dreams. The text does not describe any other responsibility, any minor services Joseph owed the two. But with this development in the narration, the framework for a plot in the scene seems to break off. Emphasis on Joseph's administration skills, clear in ch. 39, now fades. The sole focus of attention centers on the dream narration and the corresponding interpretation, not on interrelationships among the principal characters of the scene, not on Joseph's future as a prisoner. Vss. 14–15, to be sure, constitute a petition designed to facilitate Joseph's release from the prison. But even here, the petition seems to be tied directly to Joseph's skill as a dream interpreter.

The dream narration begins in vs. 5 with a general statement that the dreams occurred, parallel in structure and function to the introductory formulas in 37:5 and 9a. The dream reports then develop as an exchange between Joseph and the two servants of the Pharaoh. Vss. 6–8 contain a conversation among all three figures, designed to elicit the dream reports themselves. Joseph's explanation that dream interpretations belong to God gives Joseph's role in this scene a theological rootage, similar to the assistance formulas in 39:2–3 and 21 (cf. below on 41:16,25). Vss. 9–11 contain the dream speech of the cup-bearer, structured like the dream speeches in Gen 37. The initial call to attention is just one word, but nonetheless it carries the same catchword noted above. And it functions in the same manner: *baḥălômî*. The second part begins with *wᵉhinnēh* and details the dream.

Vss. 12–15 then follow with Joseph's interpretation and a request with its proper justification. The interpretation itself begins with a headline, *zeh pitrōnô* (cf. Dan 2:36; 4:24)[29] and develops the dream report as an allegory. Then as if building on the positive character of the interpretation, Joseph poses a request. He asks the cup-bearer to intercede before the Pharaoh for him after he is restored to power. It seems to be clear, nonetheless, that as suggested above the request is rooted in the dream interpretation and does nothing to divert the scene from its focus on the dreams.

The dream speech of the baker, vss. 16–17, is structured in just the same manner as the cup-bearer's speech. The call to attention is again "in my dream," in this case strengthened by a personal pronoun and its intensifier: *'ap-'ănî baḥălômî*. As in vss. 9–11, so here the dream narration is marked off from the call to attention by the particle *wᵉhinnēh*. And vss. 18–19 contain

---

[29] Cf. Richter, "Traum," pp. 205–206.

Joseph's interpretation, introduced with the same headline: *zeh pitrōnô*. No request arises from the interpretation. The symmetry of construction is nevertheless unmistakable. Not only do we find a parallel with the dream speeches in Gen 37, but the dream speeches and their corresponding interpretation speeches within this scene parallel each other. And that parallel is even more exact than the parallel between the dreams in this scene and Gen 37.

The scene closes in vss. 20–23 with a narration of the events that fulfill Joseph's interpretation. The narration, however, signals fulfillment of *both* dream interpretations and thus stands outside the tightly knit dream structure and its corresponding interpretation. Accordingly, the comments about dream structure in the discussion of Gen 37 seem here to be supported. Moreover, as in the first scene of the digression, so here too the principal structure of the scene itself appears in the (dream) conversation, with narration of events designed only to introduce the crucial conversation and to show its consequences. And as in the first scene, so here the closing verse sets the stage for the following scene. The cup-bearer did not remember Joseph's request.

C. The third scene develops in a noticeably different way. It does not begin with an exposition, defining the principal characters and their circumstances. Rather, it marks a transition from the previous scene only with a dating formula in vs. 1a: *wayᵉhî miqqēṣ šᵉnātayim yāmîm*. "At the end of two years, . . ." The scene thus depends heavily on some kind of narration preceding the opening formula and cannot easily be taken as an originally independent element. Moreover, the development of the scene, as I shall suggest below, assumes that Joseph was confined in prison, thus pointing to dependency on the narration about Joseph in prison in the immediately preceding scene. Indeed, by means of the opening formula the audience now knows that Joseph had been confined for an extended period of time. Through the connection of the two scenes, therefore, the final scene of the digression begins with a decided tone of despair.

The major body of the scene moves immediately to its principal topic, vs. 1b. The Pharaoh, who needs no introduction, dreams. Vs. 1ba stands as the specific introduction for a dream report, parallel to the call to attention in 37:5aa,9a (cf. 40:9b,16ba). And the catchword familiar to such introductions also appears here: *ûparʻōh ḥōlēm*. The report itself comes in vss. 1bb–4a, introduced as might be expected with *wᵉhinnēh*. The nominal construction with an active participle in vs. 1b does not alter the basic structure of the report. But it does indicate a significant change in structure over against the earlier dream speeches. This one does not appear as a speech from the Pharaoh, but as a continuation of the narration introduced in vs. 1a. With a 3.m.s. *waw* consecutive imperfect of the verb *yqṣ*, vs. 4b marks the end of the first dream report. And the second one begins in vs. 5a, with the appropriate catchword again prominent. Vs. 5b then reports the dream, with the conclusion marked in vs. 7b with the same form of the same verb from vs. 4b. The only remarkable element in the structure of the two dream reports is the dominance of participial construction that emphasizes the immediate and, perhaps, mysterious quality in the content of the dream.

The next stage of structure in the scene begins in vs. 8 with a notation of time similar to the one in vs. 1a*a*. A narrative element in vs. 8 (cf. Dan 2:2–10; 4:6–7; 5:7–8) sets the stage for the development of a movement in the scene of even more significance than the dreams. In typical fashion the Pharaoh calls his officials for interpreting dreams (cf. Dan 2:2; 4:6; 5:7). In typical fashion, the professionals can provide no clear interpretation (cf. Dan 2:10–11; 4:7; 5:8). The cup-bearer then remembers his experience with Joseph, who remains where he was when the cup-bearer left him two years earlier. And Joseph is summoned from the place, from the prison (*min-habbôr*), for an audience with the king. Before the audience, however, Joseph shaved and changed his clothes. The image is one of a man who had been confined, indeed, confined against his will. And significantly, Gen 37 provides a parallel with its report of Joseph confined against his will in a pit (cf. 37:20,24,28,29, all of which describe Joseph's place of confinement with the noun *habbôr*).

A brief conversation, with theological overtones like 40:7–8, leads to a repetition of the dream report in vss. 17–24.[30] The pattern of structure for the report remains the same as it was in vss. 1–7. But here the report is structured as a speech of the Pharaoh to Joseph. The dream speech can be divided into two parts, each structured on the same order (vss. 17b–21 and 22–24). Thus, both vss. 17b and 22a contain a typical call to attention (cf. 37:6,9), both constructed with *baḥălōmî* (vs. 22a adds *wā'ēre'*, cf. 40:16). In vs. 22b, the movement from the introduction to the body of the dream is marked by the simple particle *wᵉhinnēh,* as one would now expect. Vs. 17b is similar, although the particle has a suffix associated directly with a participle: *hinᵉnî 'ōmēd.* Both develop the dream narration with a wide variety of syntactical patterns, using especially participial construction in the body of description (cf. the comments above). And both end with a clear statement of conclusion (vss. 21b and 24b). Symmetry continues to be apparent.

Joseph responds in vss. 25–36 with his interpretation of the dream, a request, and the justification for the request (cf. 40: 12–15). The formula marking the beginning of the interpretation here is different and considerably longer than the one in 40:12: *ḥălôm par'ōh 'eḥād hû'* (cf. vs. 26b). But it obviously has the same function. The interpretation outlines seven years of fertility to be followed by seven years of famine, then suggests procedures for controlling the plight to be produced by the extended famine. Joseph suggests that the Pharaoh should establish a new administrative office, a

---

[30] Cf. von Rad, *Genesis,* pp. 370–371, 378 for comment on the theological significance of this point.

grain dispensary. One should note at this point that Joseph's interpretation and counsel derive basically from his own skill rather than from divine intervention. To be sure, he attributes his interpretation to God. But there is no direct divine intervention in the process of interpretation (contrast Dan 2:19). And the counsel following from the interpretation reflects Joseph's skill as a speaker before the king, not a part of the dream interpretation that is in some manner the result of divine inspiration.

A series of speeches from the Pharaoh follows the interpretation, one to his servants (vs. 38) and three to Joseph (vss. 39–40,41,44). The first speech to Joseph, vss. 39–40, sets out the Pharaoh's reasons for elevating Joseph to a position of power. The elevation itself is to a position over the Pharaoh's *house*, parallel to the elevation in the first two scenes. The second speech, vs. 41, contains an elevation for Joseph to a position of power over all of Egypt, and thus is a unique element in the process of Joseph's rise to power. It is this speech that places Joseph in a position of power over the grain office, the office that he himself had suggested in his counsel. Moreover, it is this elevation to office that opens the door for connection with chs. 42 and 43–45. Vss. 42–43 then narrate the elevation, with terminology drawn from ancient ceremony. But the narration is somewhat anticlimactic, adding complementary color to the major movement in the speech (cf. the comments above about major movements in the scenes of the digression accomplished through speeches or conversation). The final speech, vs. 44, also elevates Joseph to a position of power, thus duplicating the second speech (on duplicate speeches, cf. below). The speech begins with an authorization formula: "I am the Pharaoh" (cf. Lev 18:5).[31] Then by decree the Pharaoh establishes Joseph's position. The execution of the decree comes in vs. 45, with a name change, a marriage into an official family, and a statement that Joseph exercised his office. And with that report, the digression reaches its conclusion.

It should be noted here that Joseph's ability as a counselor and administrator functions as the primary reason for the Pharaoh's decision to elevate him to a position of power.[32] Joseph's interpretation speech recommends that in order to combat the years of coming famine, the Pharaoh should choose a discreet and wise (*nābôn wᵉḥākām*) man to fill storage bins during the years of fertility. These characteristics constitute the basis for the Pharaoh's decision. To be sure, the characteristics come from God. But it is Joseph's own ability that promotes him for the position: "Since God has shown you all this, there is none so discreet and wise *as you. . . ."* Thus, the reason for Joseph's elevation to a position of power is his ability to

---

[31]Cf. W. Zimmerli, "Ich bin Jahwe," in *Geschichte und Altes Testament* (*Beiträge zur historischen Theologie* 16; Tübingen: Mohr, 1953) 179–209.

[32]Contrary to J. Crenshaw, "Method in Determining Wisdom Influence Upon 'Historical' Literature," *JBL* 88 (1969) 129–137.

administer the position effectively, not to mention his perception in conceiving the office and the qualifications for it (cf. 1 Kgs. 3:3–15, especially vs. 12).[33]

The final element of structure in the scene begins in vs. 46a with a nominal sentence, noting Joseph's age at the beginning of his administration. Vss. 46b–52 then narrate events of the seven years of fertile production, including the birth of Joseph's sons. Vss. 53–57 follow with a narration of events in the seven years of famine. Joseph's interpretations have been fulfilled. But the major impact of this element lies beyond the fulfillment pattern. The entire narration, vss. 46b–57, describes Joseph's administration of the office during the years of fulfillment.

The structure of the scene's major body is, as noted above, strikingly different from the first two scenes of the digression. The speeches carrying the dream reports and Joseph's elevation to a high office are balanced by narration for the same events. And a narration for the fulfillment of the dreams brings the scene to its conclusion. Joseph's elevation to office occupies a more important role in the body of this scene than it did in the first two. Nevertheless, the focus of the structure does not fall so much on how Joseph secured his position, nor even on the events in Joseph's administration, but on the ability Joseph had for executing the office.

EXCURSUS: *The digression as a unit.*

Each one of the scenes in the digression is intricately related to the others. No part is out of place. But no intrinsic element of structure in the digression depends on the preceding or the following parts of the Joseph story. To be sure, the digression ties into the preceding crisis exposition, primarily through the last verse of Gen 37. And it makes occasional allusions to events described in the opening chapter (cf. 40:15; 41:51–52). But these ties are not structurally indispensable. Moreover, some structural symmetry ties the digression into the Joseph story. But again, the symmetry reflects a plan for the whole story, not the digression. There is no reference in any part of the digression to Joseph's bad relationship with his brothers, no sign of the Canaan—Egypt dialectic in the story as a whole. Rather, the digression introduces its own themes, its own set of keys that move in progressive steps toward a particular conclusion. Joseph begins as a servant and moves by means of his own skill as well as God's presence to a position of power in a household, in a prison, in a nation. It ends appropriately with a note that Joseph executed his office of power to the benefit of the Egyptians and all the earth.

The implication of this observation is that the digression in Gen 39–41 is

---

[33] For a more detailed analysis of this issue, cf. Coats, "The Joseph Story . . . ," p. 289–291.

basically unified. Redford, on the contrary, maintains that Gen 39 was not an original part of the Joseph story, but a written document attached by a later manipulator of the text through patched-up joins.[34] Syntactical and lexical studies, however, do not supply the major source of evidence for this conclusion, as Redford observes. The evidence derives rather from stylistic and theological observations. One point of support is theological: The name, Yahweh, appears at the introduction and conclusion of ch. 39 and reveals a unique theological stance. Since the name appears at no other point in the entire Joseph story, it argues for exclusion of the chapter.[35] But there is a problem in the observation that weakens the evidence as support for excluding the entire chapter from the story. Redford has not recognized that the chapter division does not constitute the proper structural division of the scene. The divine name appears, not at the beginning and ending of the spurned wife scene, but as parallel elements in the beginnings of two distinct scenes.[36] To eliminate the chapter at least partly on the basis of the names means to eliminate not only the spurned wife scene, but also the exposition for the prison scene. One would still be faced with the necessity for accounting for the name, Yahweh, in these texts and not in any other points of the entire story. I would suggest as a possible step toward that end that the name may have entered the story because of vocabulary patterns in the assistance formulas. But in any case, it seems to me to be clear that the pattern of divine names cannot be used as strong evidence for excluding the chapter.

A second point derives from stylistic observations, particularly of recapitulation and repetition patterns. According to Redford, recapitulation in Gen 39 is shoddy, the repetition unimaginative when one contrasts the chapter to other parts of the story.[37] Thus, vs. 8 repeats part of vs. 6 and vss. 14–15 must be set against two parallels, vss. 10–12 and vss. 17–18. But why should repetition be judged to be so bad here and not so bad in other parts? Redford feels that repetition in, for example, 41:9–12 is necessary, an effective element of style. I do not disagree with that observation. But I cannot see qualitative differences between the text in 41:9–12 and the repetition patterns in ch. 39.

Finally, Redford believes that the ending of the scene is unbelievable.[38] Indeed, if one believes that the story was originally independent, the

---

[34] Redford, pp. 146–147,181. But cf. p. 93, where he asserts that the motif about a spurned woman was never used as a self-contained narrative. John Skinner, *A Critical and Exegetical Commentary on Genesis* (*ICC;* 2nd. ed; Edinburgh: Clark, 1930), 439, presents an effective evaluation of essentially the same point in B. D. Eerdmans, *Die Komposition der Genesis* (*Alttestamentliche Studien* 1; Giessen: Töpelmann, 1908) 66–68.

[35] Redford, p. 130.

[36] Cf. Gunkel, *Genesis*, pp. 420–426.

[37] Redford, pp. 77–85.

[38] Redford, p. 92.

conclusion would be difficult to interpret. A major crisis for Joseph develops with dramatic force. Joseph is liable for a death penalty. But 39:19b–20a notes only that Joseph lands in prison. It does not say that he is free from the death penalty. The scene ends in full suspense. But it ends without a complete conclusion. Without the following two scenes, the ending is unbelievable, truncated. But as an intricate part of the digression, the scene has an excellent continuation. Joseph is confined on the basis of a false accusation. And that confinement provides a transition to the second scene. To be sure, nothing is said of a death sentence for either Joseph or the unfaithful wife, conclusions that might be expected from parallels in ancient Near Eastern literature (cf. the *Story of the Two Brothers*). With the transition, the false accusation against Joseph and the unfaithful wife responsible for sending him to prison simply drop from sight. But this observation does not suggest that an original ending *of this story* is missing. It suggests only that reference to a death penalty is not necessary. It is no longer a relevant part of the narration. My point is not to deny that some widely circulating motif or even an explicit story like the *Story of the Two Brothers* may lie behind the scene as an inspiration for the construction of this particular movement. It is to argue only that it would take a rigid and unnecessary insistence on logical execution of this narrative on the basis of the parallel motif to demand that problems in the transition from the one scene to the other be defined. Direction for analyzing the structure lies in recognizing the interdependence of the spurned wife scene and the prison scene, as well as the point of transition between the two. With the relationship between the two scenes in view, vss. 20–23 in Gen 39 do not appear to be so contrived, but simply a means for moving from one scene to the other, the conclusion of one in a full state of suspense and the beginning of the other with a proper exposition. The symmetry of construction between the two scenes would support this conclusion.

The two scenes, moreover, show no signs that they should be understood as doublets for a single scene. This question will be pursued in more detail in the following chapter, since it bears directly on the source analysis of the unit. At this point, my concern is to argue that just as the evidence does not support a conclusion that ch. 39 is a distinct literary entity, unrelated to the Joseph story digression but inserted here out of its proper context by means of weak links, so the evidence will also not support a conclusion that the chapter is a literary duplicate of ch. 40, inserted here by a subsequent redactor with distinct elements added only to provide contrast.

Perhaps the one piece of evidence pressing this point is the designation of both Potiphar in 39:1 and the captain of the guard in 40:3–4 as *śar haṭṭabbāḥîm*. It can be argued that Joseph was sold to Potiphar or the master of the prison, thus that he appears in ch. 40 not as a prisoner but as a slave. It could also be argued that the exposition to the second scene, 39:20b–23, is a poor and secondary link between two stories originally quite distinct or two copies of the same story. In that case, the second scene would begin with Joseph as the servant of the master of the prison, just as he is at the beginning of ch. 39. Then the scene would have him quickly transferred to the two officers of the prison in order to introduce the new material (cf. the structural analysis above). Again, however, the evidence is equivocal and cannot be taken as conclusive signs of two independent units or duplication of the exposition. If the position stated above should be followed, the argument would have to depend on establishing clearly that Joseph was in the prison, not as a prisoner, but simply as a slave. But in order for the scene to develop, the narration must show that the two officers of the Pharaoh were prisoners. And it was in that context that Joseph became their servant. Moreover, he becomes their servant, not simply as a slave who could be moved by his master at will, but as a fellow prisoner. This observation can be maintained in the light of 40:15b and 41:14a. Both texts make sense as allusions to Joseph's confinement in prison at the end of ch. 39. Further-more, Joseph's appeal to the cup-bearer for intercession before the Pharaoh does not imply that he wants to leave a master in favor of entering service for the Pharaoh. It implies that he wants an appeal to a higher authority in order to end his unjust confinement. Joseph was in prison (cf. 40:14b). The position implies a social stratification among the prisoners themselves. Men in the administration of the Pharaoh could command a servant, although themselves confined to prison. But the picture does not seem to me to be too farfetched, particularly in the light of current practices for confining men formerly in position of high rank. And it would facilitate the movement of the story. (Ps 105:16–22 casts an image of Joseph as prisoner, bound in iron.)

The two chapters thus cannot be defined satisfactorily as parallel entities, discrete and originally independent of each other, or copies of the same movement. To the contrary, they complement each other. They function together as integral parts of the same developing narration. It may be that two distinct traditions have been brought together in the single story, joined perhaps by the two parallel expositions. It is thus quite cogent to hypothe-size that something like the Egyptian *Story of the Two Brothers* may lie behind the construction of ch. 39 and perhaps a distinct dream interpreta-tion tradition behind ch. 40. If that is true, incidentally, would it not suggest that ch. 39 continues into ch. 41, with the dream scene in ch. 40 pinpointed as the extrinsic element?[39]

In any case, an important distinction now needs to be made. The tradition employed in the construction of this story does not enable us to conclude that the part of the story influenced by the tradition was itself once intact and distinct from the remaining scenes, any more than we can conclude that

---

[39] In the *Story of the Two Brothers,* the younger brother eventually finds himself elevated by the Pharaoh to the position of Crown Prince. Cf. *ANET*, p. 25.

those sections in Shakespeare's *Hamlet* influenced by the traditional tale were originally not a part of Shakespeare's work but independent, structured intact by Shakespeare into his drama. An earlier revenge play called *Hamlet* may very well have provided resource for Shakespeare's art. But even if that is the case, the product of his art shows his transforming touch, the work of his own creativity. The traditions that may lie behind the scenes in the Joseph story digression, traditions that may have been independent and distinct, have in the same manner been transformed into a new construction. And in that new construction, the two scenes function as intrinsic parts of the digression. No evidence that the digression existed without ch. 39 or that ch. 39 existed as an independent story about Joseph, the hero of the digression as a whole, can be found.

Traditio-historical questions confirm this observation. This unit appears to have had a life of its own before its incorporation into the body of the Joseph story, as would be suggested by the opening observations of this excursus.[40] Moreover, as a distinct story within the Joseph story, the unit is subject to its own genre analysis. I have argued in another context that these chapters should be seen as a political *legend*.[41] If the hypothesis is correct, then the frustrating penchant for developing the seeds of a plot, only to drop them without full development, would fit. Legends characteristically compromise plot development in favor of emphasis on the characteristics of the central figure.

One final note about the digression as a unit: Joseph's character in the digression seems totally different from the presentation of the same figure in Gen 37. In crisis situations, in despair and poverty, in power at all levels, he is the image of a well-disciplined leader, an ideal administrator of a powerful office. And that image is maintained in each scene of the digression. The legendary quality of the central figure thus adds to the unity of the digression and its contrast with the larger scope of the Joseph story.

IV. COMPLICATION OF PLOT (Gen 42)

Gen 42 is closely linked with the following element of structure, yet it picks up the major plot introduced in Gen 37 and carefully integrates the subplot of Gen 39–41. The internal structure of the scene, moreover, demonstrates the structural dialectic of the story as a whole. Following an exposition (A), the tension of the story compounds with the brothers moving *from Canaan to Egypt* (B). Then following a transition interlude (C), the

---

[40]Cf. Gunkel, "Die Komposition . . . ," p. 62–66. More recently, W. Lee Humphreys, *The Motif of the Wise Courtier in the Old Testament,* (unpublished dissertation, Union Theological Seminary, New York, 1970) 208–216. Humphreys treats ch. 39 as distinct both in tradition history and in source.

[41]Coats, "Joseph Story . . . ," p. 288–291.

pressure of the tension peaks with the brothers returning *from Egypt to Canaan* (D).

A. The chapter begins without syntactical marks for a new scene, and without identifying data for the principals. Only a transition to Jacob in Canaan warns the audience that the narration of events has shifted away from the Egyptian context of the digression. The opening verse nevertheless integrates this element with the subplot from Gen 41 by referring to the grain in Egypt. Jacob's speeches in vs. 1b and, with a repeated introduction, vs. 2 also presuppose Gen 41, both by a reference to grain and by an allusion to a threat of death, obviously from the famine. After explaining reasons for his request, Jacob commissions his sons for a trip to Egypt. The purpose clause following the instructions shows the pressure for the trip. There is no choice. The brothers must buy food in the face of the famine or die. Vss. 3–5 narrate the execution of Jacob's instructions from the chapter's opening speech, bringing all the brothers except Benjamin to Egypt among other Canaanites seeking food. Benjamin, as Joseph earlier, was exempted from the responsibility the other sons carried. Thus, these verses set out the necessary conditions for the scene's narration. And they reflect the structural dialectic of the Joseph story as a whole. The brothers must go from Canaan to Egypt in order to secure food.

B. The scene shifts in vs. 6a from the brothers to Joseph, marked with a nominal sentence describing Joseph's work as the administrator of the grain reserves. The brothers present themselves in humble submission before Joseph, unaware that they have thereby fulfilled Joseph's dream (vs. 6b; cf. 37:5–11). The following interview appears amid extensive narration, designed in every case to interpret Joseph's part in the exchange. Thus, Joseph's opening question, "Where do you come from?" is prefaced by a crucial observation that he had recognized his brothers but nevertheless acted like a stranger to them, spoke harshly to them (vs. 7a). The brothers' response is introduced simply with a speech formula. No commentary is needed. In this manner, the scene places special importance on Joseph's role in the interview. It is clear that Joseph intended to conceal his identity and to place the brothers under pressure. Vss. 8–9a heighten the game with another narration commentary on a Joseph speech: "Joseph recognized his brothers, but they did not recognize him. And Joseph remembered the dream he had dreamed of them." The brothers are at the disadvantage. And the point of the disadvantage comes sharply to light in vs. 9b: "You are spies!" The brothers know that the accusation is false. Yet, how could they prove their innocence when they did not know why the charge was made? But they also know that the charge is serious. It could mean death without further hearing.

There is a subtle, but important characterization of Joseph in this interview. Why did he impose such an accusation on his brothers? The repeated emphasis on the recognition motif in the introductions to Joseph's speeches demonstrates pointedly that Joseph knows who the men are. And one must assume that knowing his brothers meant that he knew that they were not spies. The emphasis on the recognition also shows that Joseph's accusation was consciously false. But why would he fabricate an accusation? Joseph uses his false accusation to set up a test, designed theoretically to determine his brothers' honesty, but subtly to secure Benjamin's visit to Egypt. But within the structure of the scene, the accusation serves to compound the tension on the brothers. It duplicates the tension from Gen 37, but with the positions of power reversed.

Thus, Joseph places his brothers on the defensive. The brothers' self-defense speech in vss. 10abb–11 emphasizes this element by its rambling, spontaneous structure. It begins with an assertion of innocence, then in inverted sentence order it identifies their purpose in the land. The next statement, connected asyndetically with the statement of purpose in the land, defines the group as brothers. The speech then concludes with two new assertions of innocence, both connected asyndetically with the preceding elements. The first is positive: "We are forthright." The second is negative: "Your servants are not spies." The rambling character of the speech emphasizes the brothers' surprise as well as the pressure involved in the charges. They are caught off guard and can only assert innocence as if it were self-evident that the charge could not apply to them. The accusation is then repeated (vs. 12) and a second self-defense speech (vs. 13) sets the same pace (N.B. the asyndeton in vs. 13a): "Your servants are twelve. We are brothers, sons of one man in the land of Canaan. And the youngest is with his father today, and one is no more." Significantly, no question elicits the information about the family. The brothers fall all over themselves in an effort to explain their origin (contrast 43:6–7).

Joseph's speech in vss. 14–16 then specifies a test. Vs. 15 particularly parallels the knowledge formula cited in vs. 33. The word $b^ez\bar{o}'t$ in both suggests a parallel function between the test designed to establish the veracity of a claim and the knowledge formula. The content of the test, framed by two oaths, is detailed in vs. 16a. One brother must return to Canaan for Benjamin while all the others remain in prison. If the brothers can produce a younger brother, a part of their story will be substantiated. And insofar as the "test" is concerned, it will provide evidence to justify the brothers' claim for innocence (cf. vss. 33–34).

Vs. 17 marks a brief passage of time (in prison for the brothers) before a second interview, vss. 18–20. In this case, no exchange of conversation appears, Joseph simply announces that the test has been changed. All the brothers except Simeon may return with the necessary food for their families in Canaan. In order to buy more food, and to secure Simeon's release, they must return with Benjamin. Vss. 21–22 heighten the tension in the scene with an exchange of conversation among the brothers. They confess their guilt in disposing of Joseph, only to have Reuben quickly flaunt his own innocence.[42] Unity among the brothers is apparently as precarious as it ever was. A narration element in vss. 23–26 builds on the irony of Joseph's incognito before the brothers. He understood their confession, yet they did not know that he understood. Joseph turns away to weep, perhaps a structural element anticipating the resolution of the story's plot (cf. the comments below). Then the test is executed. Simeon is bound before the brothers' eyes. And the others are sent on their way with their food. And unknown to them, their money for the food has been concealed in the food bags.

C. The scene shifts in vss. 27–28 to an interlude between the Egyptian element and the brothers' interview with their father in Canaan. The setting for the interlude is an inn on the journey home (cf. Ex 4:24–26). When one man opens his bag of grain, he discovers his money. But the discovery is not treated as a sign of good fortune. The response among the brothers emphasizes the fate the brothers feel in the whole scene. They do not allude to their guilt as an explanation for the mystery. The events are beyond their comprehension. They respond, not in complaint, an appeal to God to change their plight, but in lamentation before a reality as permanent and mysterious as death. (For comments on the structural importance of an interlude, cf. above on 37:15–17).

D. The scene shifts again in vs. 29a, with the brothers now before their father in Canaan. Their speech, vss. 30–34, recites the events of their interviews with the mysterious Egyptian officer. The recitation includes the brothers' self-defense speech, a combination of the two speeches in vss. 10–11 and 13, and Joseph's test speech in vss. 14–16. The citation of Joseph's speech assumes a slightly different pattern from its counterpart. Rather than reference to the requirement as a test, as in vs. 15b, here the requirement is set in a knowledge formula: "By this I shall know that you are honest men." Returning for Benjamin thus provides evidence to establish the legitimacy of their claim. Following the knowledge formula, the event that serves as evidence for their innocence is described in detail, an elaboration of the obscure $b^e z\bar{o}'t$ in the knowledge formula.

Before Jacob responds to the report, the brothers' money is discovered, with the same consequence as in the interlude at the inn. The money is not a sign of good fortune, but a sign of ill fate. Jacob's response picks up the omen. His first speech (vs. 36) is a lament over the loss of Joseph and Simeon and the threat to Benjamin. Significantly, all three points in the lament Jacob attributes *to the responsibility of the brothers*. Yet, there is no explicit indication that the brothers' deception from Gen 37 had been

---

[42] For a discussion of significance in the confession, cf. Westermann, p. 85. It seems important to note, however, that while the confession occurs before Joseph, the brothers are not aware that they have confessed to their victim. And no consequences arise from this particular act of confession.

discovered. Rather, the element belongs to the fateful consequences foisted on the family by the events in Egypt. Jacob's plight is as grievous as it was in the conclusion of Gen 37.

The description of the discovery of the money, however, poses a problem for an evaluation of unity in the chapter. Vs. 35 stands as an apparent contradiction to the interlude in vss. 27–28. There the money was discovered in only one bag. Here the money appears in the remaining bags. This problem is heightened by 43:21, a report by the brothers to Joseph's steward that all found the money in their bags at the inn. Moreover, there is a pattern in vocabulary. In vss. 27–28 two words for the food sacks appear: šaq and 'amtaḥat. In allusions to this event in 43:12, 18–23 and 44:8 the word is consistently 'amtaḥat. Moreover, the LXX translates the one use of šaq in vs. 27 with the same term as the one used for 'amtaḥat, suggesting consistency in vocabulary. Should this use not stand in contrast to vs. 35 where šaq appears consistently? Does it not suggest that unity in the narration is weak? Yet, the argument from diction depends on an emendation. The MT significantly mixes the words. Does the argument from contradiction not face similar problems? Must we assume that a narrator cannot repeat a motif like the discovery of the money as a means for heightening tension? It might be objected that in order for the narration to be consistent, the narrator could not allow only one brother to find his money at the inn. Would the other brothers not be bound by curiosity to look for their money immediately? But the situation described by the scene does not promote curiosity. It promotes a sense of fate. The brothers may well know that their money will be in the bags since the money appeared in one bag of their number earlier. But the inexorable fate sets the mood, just as Jacob knows that Benjamin will be in danger when he goes to Egypt. That kind of fate one may well want to forestall as long as possible. But it cannot be changed. And its certainty, in both cases, produces lamentation (cf. vs. 36). This observation does not remove the internal contradiction of the chapter. Neither does it offset the allusions to the event in chs. 43 and 44. But the crucial issue lies rather in evaluating contradictions as evidence for disunity. Could the contradictions reflect some other process, perhaps a free appropriation of narration lines from one scene in the development of further parts of the scene or entirely new scenes? I shall return to this problem in the following chapter.

Vs. 36 contains the climax of the scene. Jacob refuses to allow Benjamin the privilege of a journey with his brothers to Egypt. His response captures the pathos and the irony of his fate. And he laments the loss of a son, almost as if in expectation of the loss of Benjamin. Reuben offers Jacob surety for Benjamin's safe return. The surety oath is severe—his own sons for death if he could not bring Benjamin back. But the oath does not sway Jacob. Benjamin may not go to Egypt. An immediate return for more food and, of more importance, for Simeon's release is thus impossible. The crisis of the story is therefore heightened. The stage is set for the final denouement. And the scene ends in a tragic lamentation by a disillusioned old man.

This second formal complication in the structure of the Joseph story thus amplifies the primary crisis in the story's plot, a full complement to the parallel in ch. 37. But to understand the scene as a complement of ch. 37, the same movement with the positions of power reversed, raises questions about interpretation. Von Rad suggests, for example, that the test in ch. 42 was intended to determine whether the character of the brothers had changed from the time they delivered Joseph, perhaps through various circuitous routes, to a trading caravan and thus to Egypt. Moreover, the return of the money should be seen, according to von Rad, as a gesture of generosity, provoked by Joseph's genuine love for his family.[43] The structure of the scene does not support either position. The initial interview is carried on under the pressure of a false accusation, moving first to confinement of all the brothers and then of only one. The scene is thus curiously reminiscent of the false accusation against Joseph and his unjust confinement in Gen 39. Furthermore, Joseph's character comes under attack here. The brothers are caught in a torturous fate, a life and death struggle with an accusation they know to be false. But the important observation is that Joseph consciously created the torture. He recognized who his brothers were even though they did not recognize him. The story emphasizes that point by reporting the recognition twice. The test itself does not account for the structure of the scene, but is simply a motif in Joseph's speech. Its intention is not to prove a change or lack of change in the brothers but to establish the veracity of the brothers' claim to innocence. It may be that a subtle intention is to bring Benjamin to Egypt. But I cannot see sufficient evidence to suggest that an even more subtle intention is to duplicate the situation in Gen 37 *in order to see* whether the brothers would respond in the same way. Joseph's intention, or better, the narrator's intention in the test is to increase the tension of the story to its breaking point. Since Joseph obviously knows that the men are not spies, the test must be seen as a heightening of the torture. The brothers subjected Joseph to an unknown fate. Now he plays their anxiety to the hilt. To be sure, Joseph leaves the room to cry. And the cry may well prefigure the eventual break in tension in ch. 45. But at this moment in the story the cry relieves the tension only to a minute degree.

Thus the figures in the story continue their struggle against each other. A growing quarrel among the brothers (vss. 21–23) probably suggests that their character had not changed significantly from the earlier period, although the text does not appear to be especially interested in the brothers' character. In any case, the quarrel passes. And despite the break in tension suggested by Joseph's display of emotion, Joseph returns immediately to his harsh game by binding Simeon before the brothers' eyes, then sending the free ones

---

[43] Von Rad, *Genesis,* p. 384.

away. As Joseph in Gen 39, so here the brothers accused falsely of a crime face a prison sentence, and one remains in prison for an indefinite period, awaiting some kind of break in his favor. It is thus clear, so it seems to me, that Joseph in this chapter has little generosity for his brothers or his family in Canaan. The outcome of the scene leaves the family as divided as it was at the end of ch. 37.

Moreover, just as Joseph lost his freedom and found himself enslaved *in Egypt*, hopelessly *away from Canaan*, so here the brothers lose their freedom. And the loss highlights the necessity, not only for returning to Jacob with the news of yet another brother lost to the father, but also for bringing yet another favorite son into danger, *to Egypt*. The dialectic between Canaan and Egypt thus dominates the scene (cf. vss. 1–2,7,29,34), just as it does in ch. 37. And the dialectic points to the apparent irreparable break in the family. Finally, just as ch. 37 ends with a tragic lament of a father who has lost his favorite son, so here the scene ends with a tragic lament of a father who faces the loss of another favorite son. And in both cases, the father anticipates his own descent into Sheol. This scene thus adds to the complication of the plot by reversing the roles played in ch. 37. It is legitimately a renewed complication in the structure of the whole and, with element II (37:5–36), provides an effective frame for the digression.

One final comment: Joseph's character in this scene seems more nearly harmonious with the presentation of character in ch. 37. He is now a tyrannous lord, a man who uses his power to deceive, to manipulate, to antagonize, and agonize a prey. It should be noted that like chs. 39–41, ch. 42 presents Joseph as an administrator with great power. None of the Egyptians remind him of his deception in dealing with the visiting Hebrews. But unlike chs. 39–41, here he is not the ideal administrator, the man who rules his office for the benefit of all people. The contrast between the Joseph of chs. 39–41 and the Joseph of ch. 42 emphasizes the weight of Joseph's character in 42. He is now the opposite. He has become an anti-legend.

V. DENOUEMENT (43–45)

The denouement refuses to break the tension of the plot in the Joseph story very easily. To the contrary, the narration here moves the tension first to its fullest point, incorporating the crucial elements in the development of the story to this moment. The structure of the scene demonstrates the observation: Following an exposition (A) setting the brothers before their father in Canaan, the story develops the tension to a point of crisis (B). Just as they did in the previous element, so here the brothers move *from Canaan to Egypt* and confront signs of their mysterious fate. Yet, an apparent denouement occurs and the tension relaxes. With the next element in the scene, however, the tension returns (C). And the renewal of tension develops in the midst of a journey *from Egypt to Canaan*. The peripeteia (D) sets the brothers again in Egypt, with the tension developed to its breaking level before the denouement can finally be real. The last element in the scene (E) has the brothers returning from *Egypt to Canaan* with the news of the denouement for the father, in effect an anti-climax in the scene. Thus, it is in the internal symmetry of the scene as well as the symmetry of construction between this scene and the preceding ones, particularly element IV, that the artistic unity of the Joseph story can be most clearly seen.

A. The scene begins with an exposition parallel to the one in Gen 42: "The famine was severe in the land." Vs. 2a marks an indefinite passage of time between the preceding chapter and the scene now underway, time unjustly spent in prison by another member of the family (cf. 41:1). And then a conversation between Jacob and his sons in vss. 2b-14 repeats the commission motif from ch. 42: Jacob must send his sons from Canaan to Egypt in order to buy food. The commission process is more involved, however. The dialogue begins with a commission speech from Jacob in vs. 2b (cf. 42:2). The sons respond. But contrary to their response without objection in ch. 42, here Judah as the spokesman for all the brothers objects to the commission (vss. 3-5). Jacob does not answer Judah directly. Instead, he accuses all the brothers of acting irresponsibly to their father by telling the "man" that a younger brother remained at home. The brothers' defense to the charge (vs. 7) builds on *deception* as the guideline for relationships with their father. Like the situation in 37:31-32, the brothers fabricate an alibi.[44] They refer responsibility for the information they provided to a direct question from Joseph. Such a question appears in 43:27. But it does not appear in the preceding scene (cf. 50:16-17). To the contrary, in the preceding scene the brothers fall all over themselves in offering information that might meet the surprising accusation that they were spies. There was no need for Joseph to question them directly in order to gain that information. They laid it all out in their rambling, panic-stricken self-defense. And to imagine that an account of such a question has dropped out of the text seems to me to be sophomoric manipulation of a delicate literary construction.

Judah follows the play immediately with a request that Jacob send Benjamin with the convoy to Egypt. His request rests on the same life and death argument Jacob used in 42:2. There is no real choice. And in order to

---

[44] Cf. Kessler, p. 159-160. He argues that the text should not be understood to mean that the brothers lie to their father. 42:30-34 notes that the brothers had already reported the details of the interview with the "man." And in that report they confessed that they told the man of a brother at home. But again I see no contradiction that drives the exegete to seek layers in the narrative. In 43:7 the father knows that the brothers told the "man" of Benjamin. The text does not intimate that Jacob had discovered the brothers' slip. Rather, the father wants to know why the brothers told the "man" so much. And it is in that context that the alibi appears. The deviation between 42:30-34 and 43:7 arrises, not because of doubling in the story or traditio-historical layers, but because the narration skillfully depicts pressure on the brothers and thus their characteristic reaction to the pressure.

secure the request, he then provides surety for Benjamin's return with a conditioned self-curse.[45] But his speech also implies an accusation: "If we had not delayed, we would now have returned twice." The accusation is not directed to Jacob, but Jacob obviously was responsible for the delay. The tension dividing the family obviously remains.

The dialogue concludes with Jacob's new commission. The substance of the commission (vss. 11–13) details plans for making the most effective presentation to the Egyptian, including dispatch of Benjamin. Vs 14 picks up the pathos of the plot, already apparent in the complication of ch. 42. An inexorable fate hangs over the family. It is already clear that Benjamin will be under unusual danger. And nothing Jacob can do will stop it. Yet, despite the hopeless situation, Jacob blesses his sons in the name of El Shaddai. And the point of the blessing is not so much the success of negotiations for food, as for the safe return of Benjamin and "the other brother." Despite the inexorable fate clouding the scene, the blessing suggests a remarkable note of hope. And the allusion to the "other brother," obviously a reference to Simeon, echoes a subtle longing for Benjamin's own brother.

There is nonetheless a jarring impact in the contact between the blessing and the narrative context dominated by a sense of fate. It is almost as if the hopeless man hopes for the future of his children. Yet, a genuinely hopeless man can hardly build hope out of the blue. If the blessing is hopeful, we must ask about the ground of the hope. And that point is clear. Jacob's hope despite fate grounds in El Shaddai.[46] It is significant, then, that the name El Shaddai appears in Gen 17:1; 28:3; 35:11; 48:3; and Ex 6:3 in explicit relationship to the promise for great progeny. It is difficult to draw conclusions about the Joseph story on the basis of these parallels, however, since all of the parallels derive from texts that are later than the Joseph story, from P rather than the earlier tradition reflected in the Joseph story. Yet, would it not be possible to see grounds for suggesting an earlier, traditional association between El Shaddai and the promise tradition? Would evidence for such an earlier connection not be found in Gen 49:25?[46a] And if the connection were there, would the use of El Shaddai in Jacob's blessing not tie his concern for his sons to the larger patterns of promise so common in the patriarchal narratives? And would the concern for the safety of the sons not also tie this scene with 45:5–7? The appearance of the name, El Shaddai, is of course weak evidence to support such an assertion. But it

---

[45] Von Rad, *Genesis*, p. 387.

[46] Gunkel, *Genesis*, p. 449. He feels a sharp contrast between Jacob's sad resignation and the hopeful character of the blessing.

[46a] Frank M. Cross, *Canaanite Myth and Hebrew Epic. Essays in the History of the Religion of Israel* (Cambridge: Harvard, 1973) 47, n.15. In his opinion, the appearance of the name in Gen 49:25 is "sufficient evidence that P draws upon old tradition." Cross includes Gen 43:14 among the P texts. But cf. Noth, *Pentateuchal Traditions*, p. 266.

does open the door for an evaluation of additional evidence from subsequent scenes in the story. The analysis below will develop the point.

B. The next element in the scene, vss. 15-34, begins with a transition to Joseph in Egypt (vs. 15). The first movement sets the stage for a new interview between Joseph and the brothers, cast as a banquet prepared especially for them. But the scene does not develop as one might have expected from the past events. Introduced with a commentary on the circumstances that surround their reception, the brothers highlight their anxiety in a soliloquy. The mysterious invitation to the banquet they understand as a ruse to hide a trap. The occasion might be used, so they feared, to accuse them of stealing the money they paid for the grain in their previous interview with Joseph, an opportunity to reduce them all to slaves. Thus, the pressure of the tension from the previous scene still dominates the narrative. But now the tension reveals an air of mystery as well as the patterns of an uncontrollable fate. It is significant that the mysterious fate now outweighs the brothers' guilt over Joseph as an explanation for unexpected events (cf. 42:21). And so the brothers simply protest their innocence and declare their intent to pay for all they have received and all they hope now to receive. But the mystery is compounded with the steward's speech (vs. 23a). He declares the brothers innocent, confirms proper payment of the record for the previous purchase, and then restores Simeon (vs. 23b). Their fate, again attributed to God (cf. 42:28), is good, not bad.

The banquet itself extends the pattern of mystery and fate. After an appropriate question about the well-being of the father, Joseph recognizes his own brother. And the weeping motif returns. In the initial occasion for the motif, the cause for the weeping is somewhat unclear. It might have been the brothers' contentious struggle among themselves, if not simply the sight of brothers who had violated brotherly loyalty. But structurally, it served as a brief release of tension (cf. 42:24). Here, however, it is clear that the motif connects with Joseph's first sight of Benjamin, an expression of concern for his own brother. And in the motif the relaxation of tension depicted in the banquet grows stronger. Perhaps now Joseph can develop some kind of genuine compassion for at least one brother.

But in addition, the mystery is present. Joseph weeps in secret, then eats apart from the brothers. Moreover, the brothers are seated in the proper order of their birth, a mystery in itself, then served portions of the banquet from Joseph's table. But the mystery compounds once again when Benjamin receives a portion five times larger than the others. Yet, despite the mystery, the mood is a joyous one. "They drank and were drunken *with him.*"

Thus, the scene narrates an apparent climax. The mystery involving the money breaks in the brothers' favor. Benjamin provided evidence to counter the charge of espionage. Simeon was safe. The brothers were reunited. Relationships with the Egyptians were good. The time was ripe for celebrating good fortune. The fortune might not be any easier to understand than in the previous scene. But at least it was good. The business was completed successfully. And the brothers were together.

~ C. However, the climax is only apparent, the break in tension short-lived. In 44:1–13 the tension in the plot rises again, this time to a higher pitch. Joseph's first speech to his steward sets out a plan to construct false evidence for a false accusation (cf. Gen 39:13–14).[47] Money is again hidden in the food sacks. The pattern thus parallels the previous scene. But in fact, the money is rather inconsequential. Joseph also orders a silver cup placed in Benjamin's bag. The instructions are executed, the brothers dismissed, and the stage set for a hoax. Then Joseph instructs his steward to pursue the brothers with the new accusation: "Why have you exchanged evil for good?"

The brothers' response to the accusation draws on the play of mystery, of the incredible fate from the previous scene. Their speech has the same unorganized flow characteristic of 42:12. It begins with a complaint, in effect, a counter accusation: "Why does my lord speak such words as these?" But this accusation calls for no response. Rather, the brothers move immediately to their own defense. Their first line of defense calls on the obvious rather than hard evidence. They simply fall on the apparent absurdity of the accusation. Then an argument from their past good faith supports a rhetorical question: "How could we steal silver or gold from your master's house?" But the crown of a rash defense lies in the final oath, a self curse (vs. 9).[48] The brothers are convinced that the cup could not be in their baggage. So, on the basis of that conviction, they swear death for any man whose sack should conceal the cup, as well as slavery for all the others. But the oath does not stand. The steward reduces the penalty by stipulating that only the guilty brother would become a slave. None would die. Then, with masterful skill the story narrates the crisis. Quickly the bags are lowered. Slowly the steward investigates each one, from the bag of the eldest to the bag of the youngest. And the evidence, found in the last bag, incriminates Benjamin. For the brothers, the fate dominating the plot of the entire story now finds its final prey.

D. The next stage in the structure of this scene shifts the brothers back to Egypt, back before the accuser (44:14 – 45:15). It is in this element that the real peripeteia of the Joseph story appears. But even here the plot moves slowly. In parallel with ch. 42, this text stands the brothers again under a life or death charge. Judah acts as spokesman since his surety oath binds him to return Benjamin safely. His defense speech, however, does not demonstrate a flow of illogical reaction motivated by panic, but a carefully constructed

---

[47] Von Rad, *Genesis*, p. 391, observes: "During the night, Joseph gave his instructions to the steward. He is playing an insolent, almost wanton game with the brothers."
[48] Von Rad, *Genesis*, p. 392.

piece of argument. The speech begins with a supplication formula, a petition for patience, and an appeal to Joseph's position "like the Pharaoh himself" (cf. 2 Sam 14:17). With precise detail, previous conversations between Joseph and the brothers (vss. 19–23) as well as between Jacob and the brothers (vss. 25–29) serve as the basis for his appeal. Citing Joseph's dialogue with the brothers shows that the circumstances bringing Benjamin to Egypt were foisted on the brothers by Joseph, and thus were beyond the brothers' control. The Jacob dialogue shows that loss of Benjamin would spell the death of the father. Then, on the basis of this evidence, Judah founds his appeal. He, Judah, should be confined in the place of Benjamin, in order to allow Benjamin freedom to return home.

The structure of Judah's argument is crucial. Judah does not offer himself in the place of Benjamin because of a basic character trait. To the contrary, the reasons for his offer arise from the exigencies of his surrounding circumstances. The first lies in his surety oath. He had no other viable choice. To remain in Egypt as a slave would have been better than to bear the guilt of his oath for the rest of his life. The final sentence (vs. 34) rounds out the appeal with a second reason. It reflects Judah's fear for his father's life should Benjamin not return. Some degree of change in the brothers, at least in Judah (cf. Gen 37:26–27) is visible. Yet, it is a change that occurs precisely under the pressure of the brothers' plight. It is not a new character trait inherent in Judah, waiting to be uncovered by Joseph's plot. The plot itself has produced the change. It placed the brothers in a circumstance they could not control. And out of the events emerging around Joseph's plot, Judah acted, recognized the crisis. But the change does reflect Judah's decision to act in a new way, with a new commitment toward his brother.[49] Moreover, the change does not appear to me to be the intention of Joseph's plot. Joseph's intention is only to drive the tension between the brothers to its most excruciating peak. Thus, Joseph shows no concern for Simeon in prison for two years, for Jacob who could have died in the interim, for the brothers who struggled with a torturous fate. A change occurs in this scene. Compassion for Benjamin and Jacob replaces hostility and deceit. But the change occurs as if in response to a call for the future, not as an uncovering of character already effective in the past. The change is thus not the work of

---

[49] Von Rad, *Genesis,* p. 395, sees this process as a demonstration of a basic change in the brothers' character. Cf. also Westermann, p. 102. Westermann cites Judah's statement in vss. 30–31 as evidence: "Your servants will bring down the grey hairs of your servant our father with sorrow to Sheol." This point is correct. But one must be careful to evaluate the character of the change in the light of the narrative context. Only Judah steps forward. And he, significantly, is bound by a surety oath. The change is not something intrinsic in Judah's character, much less the character of all the brothers. It is a change in Judah, stimulated by the circumstances of the occasion.

any one figure in the scene. To the contrary, the change transcends the people who thought they controlled the crucial event.[50]

Joseph's contribution to the change (45:1–13) follows Judah's offer with a reversal for the entire plot of the story. Like the other important stages in the plot, this movement has some duplication of speeches. Joseph's response is introduced first by a speech with introductory commentary, instructing the attendants to leave (vs. 1). The commentary relates the speech to Joseph's problem in restraining himself: $w^e l\bar{o}'$ $y\bar{a}k\bar{o}l$ $y\bar{o}s\bar{e}p$ $l^e hit'appek$. The allusion in the phrase recalls the previous occasions when Joseph wept (42:24; 43:30) and points forward to vs. 2. The weeping characterizes an opening of passions that eventually enables the brothers to confront each other. And it is a motif that belongs primarily to the family. Joseph weeps when he confronts his brothers. He weeps after excusing himself from the brothers' view, and in this case he weeps after excusing the Egyptians. The Egyptians hear. But they remain on the fringe, uninvolved in the process. In both cases, however, the weeping orients toward the family. And it marks a break in the tension.

Joseph's instructions are carried out expressly in preparation for the crucial speech in vs. 3a and its counterpart in vss. 4b–13. The first part of the speech in vs. 3a is a self-revelation formula, the second part a question about the father. There is no reference to Judah's offer. But that is the character of the denouement. The crisis has gone as far as it can go. Joseph must either reduce Benjamin or Judah to slavery and run the risk of Judah's death or break the hoax. He chooses to break the hoax. And with the choice the air of mystery over the brothers' experiences in Egypt, projected as an inexorable fate related to guilt over initial treachery, evaporates. The plot has obviously reached a turning point.

The next stage in the scene narrates the brothers' response to Joseph's self-revelation. They flounder in dismay. Joseph may have forfeited his advantage by removing his disguise. The brothers may now understand the source of their mysterious fate. But Joseph obviously has the power. Rather than playing a game of cat and mouse, he now has the choice for disposing of his prey. As a consequence of Joseph's move, therefore, the brothers naturally

---

[50]Exegetes should guard themselves against the temptation to beatify Joseph, such as the suggestion of Charles T. Fritsch, "God was with Him. A Theological Study of the Joseph Narrative," *Int* 9 (1955) 21–34. But von Rad also succumbs to the temptation. A case in point is von Rad's treatment of Joseph's trick with the money in the food bags: "Joseph's replacement of his brothers' money in their sacks is to show that they were his guests; it is a sign of his deeply veiled love which makes them so great a gift. But this, like everything about Joseph, must be enigmatic to them at first and frighten them." So, von Rad, *Genesis*, p. 384. Unfortunately, Joseph's "love" remains deeply veiled for at least an extended period of time, leaving the brothers in mortal anxiety. For another example of the tendency, cf. Ruppert, p. 92. The tragedy of this tendency is that Joseph does not need to have his character defended. He stands as a vivid, powerful figure, the "hero" in a masterful work of literary art.

respond with a new sense of anxiety. But the reaction segment has a structural significance as well. It opens the door to a second self-revelation speech, more complex and more important than the first.

The second Joseph speech is preceded by a short set of instructions to the brothers (vs. 4a*a*), in effect, a last delay in building tension for the climax of the story. The brothers execute the instructions (vs. 4a*b*), and then the pivotal speech (vss. 4b-13) marks the release of tension crucial for the plot. Fundamentally, it demonstrates Joseph's decision, not to dispose of his prey, but to commit himself to brothers. As such a focal decision it complements Judah's move and carries the weight of the entire plot.

The first element of the speech is a self-revelation formula (cf. vs. 3a). Two principal sections follow, vss. 5-8 and 9-13. The first is constructed as an explicit response to the brothers' dismay, in effect, as an acquittal of their past violation. A pattern like the complaint—salvation oracle, or in this case, dismay—reassurance, lies at the base of the speech even though the usual formulas of a salvation oracle do not appear (cf. Gen 50:19-21). Moreover, the first section focuses on a theological interpretation of the brothers' treachery. The point of the interpretation, introduced first in vs. 5a*bb*, is that God was responsible for Joseph's move to Egypt. And twice again, in vss. 7 and 8, the point is repeated. God, not the brothers, sent Joseph to Egypt (cf. vs. 8).

This section of the speech recognizes that the principal span of tension in the plot of the Joseph story is the treacherous plan of the brothers to sell Joseph, thus, the broken family. However, the consequence of the plan, and thus the controlling scope of the Joseph story plot, was the shift in setting from Canaan to Egypt. This shift is reflected in Joseph's speech: "It was not you *who sent me here* but God." Since his statement is so crucial for the entire story, it demands careful attention. First is it not out of phase with the opening scenes of the story? At the point of the brothers' treachery against Joseph, there is no allusion to God's purpose. The brothers did intend to dispose of Joseph. They may not have intended to send him to Egypt, although even that is not certain. But they were the agents of Joseph's descent into Egypt. How, then, can the story shift the character of that event? It seems to me to be important to note that the reference to God as the actual agent in the event (vs. 8) does not imply that God arranged the brothers' treachery. It does not root in the past. Rather, given the events that emerged around Joseph, God's agency relates to intentions for the future. This point is made quite explicit by two purpose clauses. Moreover, the purpose clauses pick up themes from patriarchal theology, although explicit terminology from patriarchal theology does not appear. Thus, the first clause (vs. 5) shows God's purpose to be preservation of life "before you." *l^emiḥyāh . . lipnêkem*. The famine threatens an end of life in *Jacob's family*. Joseph's move to Egypt provides a means for preserving that family. The second clause (vs. 7) makes the point again. God sent Joseph to Egypt in order to establish a remnant (š*'ērît) for the family of Jacob, as well as to preserve great survivors (liplêṭāh g*dōlāh). The nouns in these phrases reflect the disaster of the famine. (They derive primarily from the disaster of war. Cf. Jer 23:3; 24:8; 40:11,15; 41:10; 42:2; 43:5; 44:7; 50:26; Ezra 9:14; 1 Chr 4:43; 2 Chr 36:20. Both words appear together in 2 Kgs 19:31 // Isa 37:32 and in Isa 10:20. The prophetic ring of this expression comes out again by comparing Mic 5:6-7.) But they also suggest, in the peculiarity of the Joseph story plot, a concern for Jacob's posterity (cf. Gen 32:9). God led Joseph to Egypt in order to preserve the people in Jacob's family. It is in the potential for the future, not in the treachery of the past that God's agency in the event can be seen. That leadership motif constitutes the warp and woof of the Joseph story, the focal point of the denouement. Moreover, the adjective, g*dōlāh, has a firm place in the patriarchal promise (cf. Gen 12:2). It thus seems difficult to cut the theological interpretation in this crucial speech entirely away from the patriarchal promise for a great posterity.[51]

The second section of the speech is cast as a message to be delivered to Jacob. It is introduced with a message commission formula. The message itself begins with a messenger formula (cf. Ex 7:16-17), in this case functioning in a secular context: "Thus says your son Joseph." The message then details instructions for Jacob to follow. The instructions center in moving Jacob and his entire family from Canaan to Egypt (cf. Gen 37:9-11). Moreover, the move opens into the exodus traditions. Thus, the sons will "go up" (wa'ălû), to report to Jacob, and Jacob with his people will descend (r*dāh) to Joseph in Egypt, to settle in Goshen, the scene of Israel's subsequent exodus from Egypt. And as in the exodus traditions (cf. Ex 10:9), so here the move includes sons, grandsons, herds, flocks, and all possessions. Thus, it is significant that Jacob's move is given a theological basis in vss. 9-10. The appeal to Jacob is made on the basis of Joseph's power. Joseph can provide (w*kilkaltî) for Jacob's family (cf. also Gen 50:21). And God made Joseph's position of power possible. Theological comment does not appear often in the Joseph story. But its presence here, in the most crucial speech of the entire plot, cannot be dismissed as incidental.

---

[51] Cf. von Rad, Genesis, pp. 398-399. He observes: "The terms, 'remnant' (š*'ērît) and 'survivor' (p*lêṭā) in v. 7 allude to that motif of rescue which is so thematically important for the entire narrative composition of Genesis. . . . This idea of the remnant is different from the prophet Isaiah's idea (Isa 6:13; 7:3; 10:20f; 14:32), for there it concerns preservation of a remnant of God's people, but here the deliverance of the bearer of promise from a universal human catastrophe." E. Ruprecht, "Mlṭ/plṭ," in Theologisches Handwörterbuch zum Alten Testament, ed. E. Jenni and C. Westermann (München: Kaiser, forthcoming), argues against this position. One would have to ask, according to Ruprecht, what larger whole the remnant survives from. He prefers to see these terms as references to the Egyptians. Yet, the entire focus of the scene presupposes the disaster caused by the famine, not only for Egypt, but for all the peoples of the world. The terms are dictated out of the context of such a disaster. Significantly, Ruprecht must eliminate one lākem in this verse. The series built on the collocation that includes lākem emphasizes to the contrary that the remnant belongs to Jacob.

The message to Jacob breaks off at vs. 11, with a final set of instructions to the brothers in vss. 12–13. With the end of the speech, the text reports that Joseph kissed his brothers, wept again, and then the group talked together. The contrast between this narration and the note at the end of the exposition in 37:4 is obvious. "After this, the brothers talked with him." "When his brothers saw that their father loved him more than all his brothers, they hated him, and could not speak peaceably to him." The tension in the family obviously has now been resolved. The brothers are reconciled.

The Pharaoh's speech in vss. 16–20 extends the peripeteia. Joseph's speech reversed the direction of the plot drastically. Now the Pharaoh's speech gives the move made by Joseph's speech additional hearing, as if to add official sanction to the reconciliation. Yet, the Pharaoh is at best a supporting character in the plot, not a principal in the action. Just as the Pharaoh's house heard Joseph's weeping without being directly involved in the reconciliation process (45:2), so now the Pharaoh adds his instructions for bringing Jacob and his family to Egypt without being directly involved in the process. His response is thus virtually an anti-climax.

The speech itself has an obvious structural problem. Cast as an address to Joseph with a message for the brothers, it has two major parts (vss. 17–18 and 19–20). It begins at vs. 17 with a message commission formula, although no messenger formula introduces the content of the message. Rather, the message begins with a brief imperative: zō't 'ăśû. "Do this. . . ." And the Pharaoh's instructions to the brothers follow. The instructions break at vs. 19 for another message commission formula, particularly if one should read the LXX *enteilai* in the place of MT ṣuwwêtāh. Then introduced with the same brief zō't 'ăśû, a second set of instructions to the brothers appears. The two sets of instructions are doublets, at least to some extent. And they illustrate the stylistic penchant noted above for doubling elements at crucial stages in the narration. The first set instructs the brothers to return with their food to Canaan, then to bring their father and their families to Egypt. The reason follows. The second speech follows the same pattern, but introduces a gift of wagons to be used in bringing Jacob and his families to Egypt. And again the reason: The Pharaoh will give them land for support during the famine.

This element of the scene ends in vss. 21–24 with a notation that the instructions were executed according to the Pharaoh's stipulations. At least one of the motifs from earlier sections of the story plays into the conclusion. Joseph gives his brothers gifts. But Benjamin receives more. At the same time, Joseph sends gifts to his father, including grain for the journey to Egypt. The first expedition from Canaan to Egypt produced grain free of cost. But the gift was colored by the burden of an inexplicable fate. Now the second expedition produces grain. But in this case the grain is a sign of the reconciliation. And it facilitates the move of all the family from Canaan to Egypt. Vs. 24 closes the element with a masterful stroke. Joseph admonishes his brothers not to quarrel on the return journey. Although the family is reconciled, the character of the brothers has not changed.

E. The final element of the unit appears in vss. 25–28. Following a transition in place, the brothers stand before Jacob in Canaan. Their speech is a report of events in Egypt (cf. 42:30–34). But it does not cover the entire scope of the events that occurred there. It sketches only Joseph's self-revelation, the point of climax for the entire plot. Thus, once again the denouement is extended. Vss. 26–27 narrate Jacob's response, with no indication about a break in the brothers' deception of their father. The point is no longer at issue. To the contrary, the family has now been reconciled, even though the possibilities for reconciliation had appeared to have been eliminated. The father receives the news, as well as the supporting evidence. And he responds with joy (cf. 46:30). He will go to Egypt. The old man will see Joseph. Thus, the scope of the story is established: Jacob in Canaan— Israel in Egypt.

VI. CONCLUSION (46:1–47:27)

Element VI in the structure of the Joseph story develops the resolution of tension from element V to a full conclusion, a completion of the multiple facets in the body of the story. It is thus an anticlimax, but fully an element in the primary structure of the story. In this element is Jacob's move, with his families, from Canaan to Egypt. Here appears the reunion between Jacob and Joseph, here Jacob's final settlement under Joseph's protective care. Significantly, the fundamental structural device for the element is an itinerary, a system of movement for the principal figures.

Moreover, no part of the scene can be separated from the Joseph story as an independent and unrelated tradition. All parts of the scene depend on the scope of the Joseph story at some part in its history. The scene is nevertheless composite, with the itinerary serving on occasion as a frame to embrace a series of secondary items: the theophany report in 46:1b–4, the name list in 46:8–27, and the administration report in 47:13–26. The theophany report and the name list anchor firmly in this element of the story, embraced by elements of the itinerary and functioning as commentary on the general character of the story. The administration report, on the other hand, stands at the end of the itinerary as an isolated unit, encompassed by two parts of the concluding statement in the story.[52]

A. The scene opens with an itinerary formula (vs. 1), composed as in the wilderness traditions with two elements. Vs. 1aa notes Israel's departure with all of his possessions without specifying a site of departure. Vs. 1ab then announces his arrival at Beer-sheba. Moreover, as in the wilderness itiner-

_____

[52] It nonetheless maintains some contact with the Joseph story, as illustrated in the opening verses. Cf. von Rad, *Genesis*, p. 409.

ary, so here the itinerary formula does not appear to be intrinsically connected with the following narration. It provides rather a piece of framework for encompassing the narration, a means for marking movement.

B. The theophany report, vss. 1b–4, employs stylistic devices, as well as elements of tradition, that appear at no other point in the Joseph story.[53] These include terminology out of the patriarchal tradition, such as "the God of your father," or "the God of his father Isaac," an explicit reference to the patriarchal promise (gôy gādôl) from Gen 12:2, direct speech from God, sacrifice, and appearance of "night visions" as distinct from the dreams of Gen 37 and 40–41 (cf. Zech 1:7–8). Vs. 1b introduces the theophany with a narration of Jacob's pious sacrifice at Beer-sheba. But the theophany itself centers, not on a description of God's appearance, but on a series of speeches. The first speech functions as a call to attention, a twice repeated call of Jacob's name. Jacob responds, typically with a single word: hinnēnî. "Here am I!" Then the primary speech begins with a self-revelation formula, relating the divine speaker directly to patriarchal traditions (cf. Ex 3:6). The principal content of the speech comes in God's admonition to Jacob not to fear, followed by a promise for God's assistance. First is an explicit pronouncement about the patriarchal promise (vs. 3bb). Vs. 4aa is structured like the assistance formula, but orients in this particular case toward Jacob's descent into Egypt. Vs. 4ab then promises the exodus at God's direction (cf. the verb 'a'alkā). And the promise ends with a stipulation about Jacob's death, to be attended by Joseph. From Canaan to Egypt. From Egypt to Canaan. Thus, although style and tradition break out of the pattern in the Joseph story, the report bears directly on the Joseph story plot.

Redford believes that a direct contradiction with the Joseph story appears at just this point.[54] This element pictures Jacob's descent into Egypt as a permanent move, while the Joseph story, so Redford argues, presupposes that the move is temporary. But the argument misses two important points. First, the move to Canaan in vss. 1b–4 is depicted as permanent for Jacob. Jacob will die in Egypt. But it is not permanent for Jacob's descendants. Second, the Joseph story is curiously silent about the length of Jacob's sojourn in Egypt. The cause for Jacob's move lies in the famine. When the famine ends, the door would theoretically open for a return. But the story does not indicate that Jacob himself will move back to Canaan at the end of the famine. The theophany report in 46:1b–4 is secondary in the Joseph story. But it is not contradictory. Indeed, it provides an early heuristic tool for interpreting the Joseph story. It indicates that, at least for the theophany report, the Joseph story is primarily focused on Jacob's descent into Egypt as a conclusion to the patriarchal traditions, a preparation for the exodus.

C. Vss. 5-7 continue the itinerary chain from vs. 1a. Vs. 5a notes Jacob's departure from Beer-sheba, although a distinctive verb appears in the element. Vss. 5b-6a define the participants in the journey (cf. Ex 10:9; 12:37), with vs. 6a noting arrival in Egypt. Vss. 6b-7 then emphasize Jacob's families as partners in the arrival. The dialectic from Canaan to Egypt now opens the door for Jacob's descendants to become Israel, in keeping with the promise for a great nation (cf. also the role of the family in Joseph's speech, 45:4b-13). But it also provides transition to the name list in vss. 8-27.

D. The name list begins with a stereotyped formula: "These are the names . . ." (cf. Ex 1:2; Num 13:15).[55] The formula then defines the content of the list: ". . . the sons of Israel who came to Egypt, Jacob and his sons." Structure in the list is controlled by stereotyped conclusions, dividing the list into four groups: sons of Leah, sons of Zilpah, sons of Rachel, and sons of Bilhah. Moreover, the conclusions regularly note the total number of the group. The Leah group includes a daughter; although the daughter is necessary to complete the number of the Leah group and finally the number of the whole unit, the allusion also picks up the story in Gen 34 and suggests that the name list has not only the Joseph story in view, but a larger collection of patriarchal traditions.

The order of the groups, and of names within each group, develops on the basis of a traditional series. Although the order of the groups in relationship to each other can vary widely, the Leah group is traditionally first. Within each group, the order of names is more tightly controlled (cf. Gen 29). Thus, in this list Joseph holds a traditional position despite the contradiction it creates with the introduction of the list (contrast Ex 1:2-4). To resolve the tension, the list concludes with two separate notations. One contains the number of the people encompassed by the list in accord with the introduction, thus excluding Joseph and his sons (vs. 26). The other is the total number of people in the families of Jacob, including Joseph and his sons (vs. 27). It is clear, therefore, that a traditional list has been adapted for this position in the Joseph story. And in this position, by providing particular details, it facilitates the description of Jacob's move from Canaan to Egypt.

Structure in each entry of the list supports this observation. Each entry contains at least an introduction: "The sons of Reuben . . . ," and a list of the sons (cf. Ex 6:14-16). The entry for Judah (vs. 12) includes, in addition to the introduction and list, an allusion to the story in Gen 38, thus demonstrating that the list has been adapted not only for the Joseph story but for the Joseph story expanded with additional material about Jacob and his family (cf. also vs. 15).The entry for Asher breaks the pattern by including a reference to a daughter and a list of sons for one of Asher's sons, although the reason for the break is obscure. The most remarkable change in the pattern comes in the Rachel group, where Rachel is included along with her

---

[55] Cf. the comments on this list above.

sons as a distinct entry (vs. 19). Moreover, the pattern in the entry for Joseph (vs. 20) is unique, with an allusion to Gen 41:50–52. Thus, by breaking the stereotyped pattern at crucial points, the list shows its special position in the Joseph story.

E. Vss. 28–30 in ch. 46 pick up the itinerary framework of vss. 1a and 5–7 with a narration of Jacob's arrival in Goshen and reunion with Joseph, and thus open the principal narration of the anticlimax. The reunion description in vss. 28–29 parallels the crucial reconciliation section in 45:14–15 and highlights the character of the conclusion as a reconciliation of the family. Moreover, the speech in vs. 30 recalls the Jacob speech in 45:28 and provides thereby additional structural unity between this scene and the denouement of the plot. One should also note that, while the allusion to Jacob's death in vs. 30 also establishes some point of contact with the framework narrative in Gen 47:38–50:14, the contact is not structural. It does not, therefore, support a suggestion that the framework narrative should be restructured as part of the Joseph story.[56]

The narration in this scene continues in 46:31–47:10 with a description of an audience between Jacob with his family and the Pharaoh. But the description reflects a problem. The first section of the narration concerns only an audience for the brothers (46:31–47:6). In the first speech in the element Joseph instructs his brothers for their role in the audience. Constructed initially as a series of three citations drawn, not from the past, but from anticipation for the future, the speech outlines the coming developments in the audience. Joseph tells his brothers what he himself will say to the Pharaoh. But his observation about profession (vs. 32) reveals the problem. It begins with a nominal sentence, specifying the men as shepherds (*rō'ê ṣō'n*), but continues with a dependent clause, introduced by *kî*, specifying the men as keepers of cattle (*'anšê miqneh*). The contradiction develops in the following parts of the audience. Joseph next anticipates the Pharaoh's response and instructs the brothers about their speech. They should say that from youth they have been keepers of cattle (*'anšê miqneh*). His speech ends with a statement of purpose in the instructions, as well as a reason for constructing the speech in a particular way. The purpose is to secure the Pharaoh's permission to settle in Goshen. But the reason for defining the profession only as keepers of cattle is a saying: "Every shepherd [*rō'êh ṣō'n*] is an abomination to the Egyptians." The implication of the counsel is that the brothers should avoid offending the Pharaoh by avoiding reference to their experience as shepherds. The contradiction between this point and Joseph's citation of his introduction suggests that the speech has been adapted in order to include the saying.

The development of the narration in 47:1–10 supports this observation. The first speech, Joseph's announcement to the Pharaoh that the families of

---

[56] Against Redford, p. 28. Cf. Coats, "Redactional Unity . . . ," pp. 19–20.

his father have arrived, notes that the brothers have flocks, herds, and all possessions with them. But contrary to the citation in 46:31–32, Joseph makes no reference to their profession. The text then narrates presentation of five brothers, with the Pharaoh's question as anticipated the first move of the audience. The brothers respond. But their speech is contrary to Joseph's recommendation. They define their occupation as shepherds (rō'ēh ṣō'n), with no reference to keepers of cattle. This development must have been the original line of the narration. Moreover, the audience itself is germane for the Joseph story as a whole, for the result of the audience is official permission to settle in Goshen. Vss. 4–6 make this point quite explicit. The brothers pose a specific request for the royal approval, and the Pharaoh agrees. In these verses, then, the descent into Egypt reaches its goal. The settlement can be completed.

Vss. 7–10 constitute a distinct section of the audience narration, Joseph's presentation of his father to the Pharaoh. Vs. 7 marks the presentation, with Jacob's blessing for the Pharaoh an immediate consequence. The exchange of dialogue in vss. 8–9 centers on a point of curiosity, Jacob's age. The age intensifies the blessing for the Pharaoh, since an older man at the end of his career stands in the most advantageous position to give blessing (cf. Gen 48). Finally, the scene narrates the blessing motif again, the crucial element of the scene and the consequence of Jacob's move to Egypt.[57]

Vss. 11–12 compose a concluding statement for the Joseph story, an account of Jacob's final settlement in Goshen under Joseph's provision and protection. Jacob's move to Egypt is now complete. (N.B. the specification of the place for Jacob and his family in vs. 11, not as Goshen, but as Rameses. Cf. Ex 12:37a.) The conclusion needs only the formulas of vs. 27a.

F. The final section of secondary tradition in this scene appears between the two parts of the story's final narration, in 47:13–26. Its position in the story is thus secured by dividing the conclusion into two parts, a procedure distinct from recapitulation. The narration begins with a brief exposition, defining the setting as the famine that brought Joseph to power in Egypt, and the principal character as Joseph, the administrator of the grain reserves. No reference to Jacob or the brothers can be found. The unit thus has more in common with the digression in ch. 39–41 than with the immediate context. Yet, it functions in a quite distinct way. It does not intend to present Joseph as a discreet and wise administrator.[58] To the contrary, it builds an aetiology for a perpetual tax system in Egypt. To that end two distinct elements of dialogue between Joseph and the people appear, each patterned as a business negotiation. The people request that Joseph sell them grain. Joseph responds by setting the price. And the text narrates the

[57]Cf. Wolff, p. 157.

[58]Gressmann, p. 2, and Humphreys, pp. 216–221, suggest that these verses belong better after ch. 41. But cf. Gunkel, "Komposition . . . ," p. 66.

consequences (vss. 17,20–22). All the land now belongs to the Pharaoh. And the people have been reduced to slaves. The one exception in the scope of the consequences is the priesthood. This total slavery to the state is made practicable by Joseph's program in vss. 23–24, a proclamation of law in the land of Egypt. The Pharaoh will give the people land, as well as seed for their crops. In return he expects a fifth of their income. Reducing the people to total slavery means that the people must pay a twenty percent income tax. The people agree, and the narration concludes in vs. 26 with a formula confirming the legitimacy of the tax for successive generations. "So Joseph made it a statute concerning the land of Egypt to this day."

This section of narration makes no real contribution to the Joseph story, focusing instead on a facet of administration within the Egyptian structure. Moreover, its aetiological character, oriented toward royal taxation, is intrinsic for the narrative, suggesting that these verses function primarily as aetiology. At least the aetiological character sets the unit apart from the rest of the Joseph story, even from the administration reports in ch. 41. On this basis, the unit appears to me to be isolated and extraneous to the overall story.

G. Vs. 27a, the end of the conclusion element from vss. 11–12, is constructed in exact parallel with the opening sentence of the Joseph story, Gen 37:1, as was argued above in the discussion of the exposition of the entire narrative. Vs. 27b introduces a distinct theme. Jacob and his people not only settle on the land, but increase in number and power, a motif which sets the stage for the exodus (cf. Ex 1:7). On the relationship between this half-verse and the remaining parts of the conclusion, cf. the discussion below.

SUMMARY

Two conclusions can be formulated as the result of this structural analysis. 1) With the exception of Gen 38 and 47:13–26, along with some secondary commentary, the Joseph story shows remarkable unity. Each of the major structural elements develops clear functional cohesion with all other parts of the whole. Following the exposition with its presentation of the principal figures and the points of tension that bring them into conflict with each other, a detailed description of the tension's scope sets the tone of the narrative. A broken family faces the tragedy of jealous hatred, violent attack, and exile for the victim from Canaan to Egypt. Then with a digression to show the rise of Joseph to power in Egypt, a second display of the story's scope of crisis puts the pressure points in the tension at the opposite poles. The two elements of complication also form a frame around the digression that integrates its motifs into the flow of the narrative as a whole. The impact of the complication elements is to project responsibility for the broken family onto no single figure, but rather to embroil all members of the family equally in a tragic struggle. The next element brings the tension to a denouement, creating the context for reconciliation when virtually no prospects for reconciliation had previously been possible. The reconciliation theme, moreover, provides the occasion for completion of a structural dialectic characteristic for the entire story: The break in the family opens with Joseph sold as victim from Canaan to Egypt. The tragedy then reaches a point of resolution when the broken family finds reconciliation in Egypt, with the entire family moved from Canaan to Egypt. The final element ties up all the lines of the narration, with the family actually transferred to Egypt. None of these elements can be dropped as duplications without seriously impairing the artistic quality of the story. Indeed, even the secondary additions to the story merge with the plan of unity in the narrative.

2) The principal structural focus of the story pinpoints the shift in setting from Jacob in Canaan to Israel in Egypt. This shift cannot be divorced from the perspective of patriarchal traditions. The promise for a great posterity lies at the basis of the procedure, at the basis of God's leadership in moving first Joseph, then Jacob to Egypt. Neither can it be divorced from the exodus traditions. In Egypt Jacob's family grows to a numerous people, only to face a Pharaoh who did not know Joseph (cf. Ex 1:8). The story as it is now formed functions basically and substantially as a bridge between two major themes of Pentateuchal traditions. It can therefore hardly be taken as an isolated piece of narrative, inserted secondarily into its present context.

CHAPTER 2

SOURCE CRITICISM IN THE JOSEPH STORY

I. METHODOLOGICAL PROBLEMS

The Joseph story as it now stands demonstrates remarkable internal unity, as well as structural and theological ties with its context. Some evidence of secondary additions to the story does appear. But even those additions do not generally impair the sense of unity in the story. They serve rather as complementary commentary. The Joseph story has nevertheless maintained a place of honor among Old Testament scholars as a showcase of evidence to support a division between J and E. This division demands attention in this chapter, not only for the sake of traditional procedure in any Pentateuchal question, but also for the sake of the primary question in the monograph. If the Joseph story in its final form serves as a bridge between the patriarchs and the exodus for the structure of the Pentateuch as a whole, what can be said about such a crucial structural function in J and E? Do both have a Joseph story? Does the Joseph story serve both in the same way? The question is a pressing one since P does not have a Joseph story, with the exception of minor elements that may be simply priestly additions to the older material.[1] Moreover, the traditional shift from the patriarchs to the exodus in the credo tradition makes no reference to Joseph (cf. Dt 26:5–6; Jos 24:4–5. Contrast Ps 105:17). It is thus crucial to know whether the bridging between the patriarchs and the exodus by means of the Joseph story appears in both J and E or only in the one or the other.

There are, nonetheless, initial problems with the traditional division. Von Rad observed:

> "The text of these chapters, apart from unimportant sections from the Priestly source, is an artful composition from the representations of the sources J and E. Apparently both documents contained a story of Joseph. The redactor combined them with each other in such a way that he inserted extensive sections of the Elohistic parallel version into the Yahwistic story of Joseph and thus created an even richer narrative."[2]

R. N. Whybray challenged this position on *prima facie* grounds.[3] He argued that the structure of the Joseph story cannot be satisfactorily explained as

---

[1] Priestly material has been traditionally identified in 37:1–2; 41:46a; 46:6–7(8–27); 47:27b–28. Cf. Noth, p. 18.

[2] Von Rad, *Genesis*, p. 348.

[3] R. N. Whybray, "The Joseph Story and Pentateuchal Criticism," *VT* 18 (1968) 522–528. Cf. also Odil Steck, *Die Paradieserzählung. Eine Auslegung von Genesis 2, 4b - 3, 24.* (*Biblische Studien* 60; Neukirchen: Neukirchener Verlag, 1970) 120, n. 291; Rainer Kessler, *Die Querver-*

the result of an interweaving of two distinct sources since the sources reconstructed out of the story have less unity, less artistic structure individually than does the whole. How can one imagine that a story of artistic mastery is the product, not of a creative artist, but of a creative redactor who builds his art from pieces of two pre-existent stories?

It is difficult, unfortunately, to explore the implications of Whybray's argument because, as it seems to me, discussions of source critical problems tend to flounder in a methodological morass. The problem is especially critical now because Pentateuchal critics do not commonly spend time in self-conscious examination of methodology for source analysis, or even extensive examination of criteria for making particular source analyses. Wolfgang Richter, an exception to the rule, has helped to identify the extent of the problem. He noted that of the three principal kinds of criteria basic for source analysis—style, contradiction in the development of narration, doublets—two must be judged as weak evidence.[4] Stylistic analysis presupposes a careful control of the peculiarities in an author's work. In the Yahwist, for example, style can be relatively well defined. It is thus quite possible to identify where the Yahwist's hand is present. But the opposite side of the coin is more problematic. A break in style may mean that a new source is present. But it may also mean that the same source now employs traditional language for a particular genre of material, language stamped by long oral usage and thus outside the realm of the Yahwist's peculiar control.

The problem is apparent in the argument for a distinct source from vocabulary. If in the middle of a Yahwistic section a word appears that does not normally belong to J, the verse cannot thereby be deleted from the J unit. It might well be that the word appears in traditional language or a particular genre J has employed. Moreover, the amount of material attributed to the Yahwist represents a problem, a problem more intensely felt in discussion of the Elohist. A significant word, rarely attested in J but present in other sources, might well be the one piece of evidence to establish J's use of the word. The point is not that a convincing argument can be made about J's vocabulary on the basis of one word. The point is that a single word cannot be used to deny a verse to J. An argument from vocabulary cannot serve as the *decisive* appeal for making source distinctions, especially when the word under question appears in a limited number of texts.[5]

---

weise im Pentateuch. Überlieferungsgeschichtliche Untersuchung der expliziten Querverbindungen Innerhalb des vorpriesterlichen Pentateuchs (unpublished dissertation, Heidelberg, 1972) 146, n. 1; Tryggve N. D. Mettinger, *Solomonic State Officials. A Study of the Civil Government Officials of the Israelite Monarchy* (*Coniectanea Biblica;* OT Series 5; Lund: Gleerups, 1971) 153–154; Paul Volz and Wilhelm Rudolph, *Der Elohist als Erzähler. Ein Irrweg der Pentateuchkritik?* (*BZAW* 63; Giessen: Töpelmann, 1933) 145–179.

[4]Wolfgang Richter, *Die sogenannten vorprophetischen Berufungsberichte. Eine literaturwissenschaftliche Studie zur 1 Sam 9,1–10,16, Ex 3f und Ri 6,11b–17.* (*FRLANT* 101; Göttingen: Vandenhoeck und Ruprecht, 1970) 58ff.

[5]George W. Coats, "A Structural Transition in Exodus," *VT* 22 (1972) 134.

An argument from contradiction faces similar difficulties. A critic of modern literature can expect narration of a plot without contradictions. But literature from the ancient world may well reflect a different standard for handling contradictions. This point is particularly important in dealing with narration formed through generations of oral transmission. In such cases contradictions can be maintained within the scope of a single narration without resolution of tension. Thus, contradictions do not *necessarily* mean that two different sources are present. They may signal nothing more than a wedding of two stages in the history of tradition. But even in narrative material that reveals the work of more studied composition, standards for consistency or concern for contradiction may not follow the same guidelines of current literary art. Source critics must be careful to determine whether what they think might be a contradiction is in fact contradictory to the flow of the narration. It is, of course, clear that contradictions may occur and may indicate source combination. One should not be blind to contradictions, or dismiss them out of hand. Yet, neither should one impute contradictions to the text if the flow of the narrative can be understood in other ways. One should not assume that a narrative must have contradictions derived from source redaction.

Richter suggests that the most reliable criterion for source analysis is the doublet. Yet, even here difficulties arise. A doublet can be a genuine indication of duplicated narration lines, and thus of two sources. There is little possibility for doubt, for example, that the doublets of the Moses' vocation account in Ex 3:1–4:18 and 6:2–7:6, can be explained most adequately as the work of two distinct and parallel sources. But duplications can serve as stylistic emphasis as well. A source critic must attempt to distinguish between doublets that function as tools for stylistic emphasis, doublets that reflect growth in the tradition preserved by a single source, and doublets that derive from the combination of two sources.

These problems have produced a cacophony of conflicting voices in discussions of Pentateuchal texts. Without careful evaluation of criteria, different scholars working on the same texts come to widely different conclusions about their literary subject. A case in point lies in the work of Georg Fohrer.[6] Fohrer's analysis of the exodus traditions begins in Ex 1:1–14 with a division into four sources, J, E, N, P. But the criteria used for defining those sources break down.[7] The methodological difficulty, however, is more extensive than a discussion of the unit in Ex 1:1–14 would suggest. All of Fohrer's commentary builds on the analysis of the initial chapter. If, therefore, the criteria Fohrer employs for making his source analysis in the first chapter break down, if that evaluation can be sustained, then the division of the text in the remaining sections of the book will also prove

---

[6] Georg Fohrer, *Überlieferung und Geschichte der Exodus. Eine Analyse von Ex 1–15* (*BZAW* 91; Berlin: Töpelmann, 1964).

[7] So, Coats, "Transition . . . ," pp. 133–134.

weak. Fohrer's form-critical and theological commentary on the following chapters may be quite perceptive. But given the difficulties in the source division, I cannot even begin an evaluation of those points. It is as if Fohrer is at work on an exegesis of a completely different text from the one that constitutes the basis for my response, although both of us may claim our literary subject to be Ex 1-15. Moreover, the problems proliferate when students adopt any particular criteria and corresponding analyses without careful evaluation.[8] The results are that families of source analysis tradition begin to appear, each carrying on their own private discussions. And the participants in the larger "discussion" ramble past each other like trains in the night, rarely if ever approaching a common point of departure.

This confusion over the text subject for exegetical discussion calls for some kind of procedure in making source distinctions that would offer control for judging doublets, contradictions, and stylistic shifts, a procedure that would offer some degree of objective operation open for all who approach a Pentateuchal text. I suggest two points as a foundation in the discussion.

A. The first point is perhaps too painfully obvious to be worthy of explicit detail. Yet, it seems to be an issue in several discussions. The point is that the MT should constitute the basic subject for exegesis. The point of departure is thus not a reconstruction of a Yahwistic text, or an Elohistic text, or a nomadic text. Rather, the point of departure should be the MT in its final form, the received text. The presupposition behind this point is that the MT is a unified and consistent text open for exegesis as it stands *unless* firm evidence proves to the contrary that it comprises two or more sources or requires reconstruction. It would therefore be inappropriate methodology, so it seems to me, to assume from the beginning that any given text in the Pentateuch is composite, with the primary task a division of the composition into its various parts. Rather, one should assume methodologically that the text he may want to analyze is a literary unity. Moreover, since the MT now stands in a unified form, it is not necessary to prove the literary unity. The burden of proof would lie on the opposite argument. It would be necessary to prove, should the evidence warrant such a belief about any given text, that the text reflects a synthetic unity composed of two or more distinct textual layers.

It might be helpful here to distinguish between various kinds of conclusions available, should the evidence suggest a composite text. a) Does the evidence point to two or more complete and parallel narrations of the tradition preserved in the received text? This conclusion would be synchronic in character, although it may have diachronic implications. b) Does the evidence suggest that a basic narration has been expanded in various editions? This conclusion would be diachronic. Only the final edition would

---

[8]Cf. H. Schmid, *Mose. Überlieferung und Geschichte* (*BZAW* 110; Berlin: Töpelmann, 1968).

be preserved in the received text, although that edition would give signs of an earlier stage of the same narration. The diachronic character of both alternatives would set the stage for tradition history studies, opening the possibilities for exploring the history of tradition behind its written edition to its origin in oral transmission. c) Does the evidence support a reconstruction in order or even sense patterns?[9] This pursuit is highly hypothetical and, in my opinion, should be followed only when strong textual evidence from the manuscripts or early versions supports the conclusion.

B. But how, practically speaking, does one proceed with an analysis that takes the final form of the text seriously, yet holds the procedure for distinguishing among various sources lying behind the final form of the text as a viable and necessary task? The normal procedure in discussion of Pentateuchal texts has been to submit the text under discussion to source analysis first, then to structure and genre questions, finally to tradition history and theological exegesis.[10] But to follow that procedure is to beg the question about unity in the text, indeed, the question about the distinctive character of the sources. If one moves immediately to the source question, the final form of the text never constitutes the subject for exegesis. The subject text from the beginning would be a reconstruction of J or P or E/N/L. And the criteria for identifying the sources would come, in the final analysis, from previous definitions of what the sources should look like. To say that any group of verses cannot belong to J because they contradict the style or world view normally attributed to J is an important argument. But it is essentially a circular argument, identifying a particular example of J on the basis of a preconceived definition of J.

As an alternative procedure, a control for the three classical criteria and a procedure open to some degree of objectivity, I suggest that discussion of any Pentateuchal text should begin with an analysis of structure in the final form of the text. Then arguments for distinct literary sources, for successive literary editions of a single source, or for reconstruction of an original text on literary grounds could be evaluated against the structure of the received text. If a suggested source distinction violates the structure of the text, if it produces two fragmented structures from a structure that in the final form of the text was well unified, the analysis should be called into serious question. This procedure would not obviate arguments from style and consistency. To the contrary, it would complement those criteria. But it would also provide control for stylistic and consistency arguments in a framework of a clearly recognizable text open for exegesis.[11]

The Joseph story provides a laboratory context for exploring the validity

[9] Cf. Redford, pp. 1-14.

[10] So, Gene M. Tucker, *Form Criticism of the Old Testament* (Philadelphia: Fortress, 1971) 42.

[11] Cf. the comments about assumptions of unity in literary criticism by Leland Ryken, "Literary Criticism of the Bible: Some Fallacies," in *Literary Interpretations of Biblical*

of this procedure, as well as its results *vis à vis* a long history of source criticism. Since the structural analysis has now been set out in detail, the argument in this chapter can turn to an evaluation of evidence. My assumption for this argument must be clear. The story stands as a unit in at least one stage of its history. The burden of proof lies therefore on the person who wants to argue that the unity is synthetic. My procedure calls, then, not for an exploration for new evidence to define unity in the text, but rather for an evaluation of evidence advanced in the past as support for an argument that would define the unity as synthetic.

II. SOURCE ANALYSIS

A. *Two parallel sources.* Gen 37 is crucial for source analysis in the Joseph story since much of the argumentation for source divisions in subsequent chapters depends on the foundation observations established here. A principal element in the argument draws on a series of doublets. Joseph's father appears as Israel (vss. 3,13) and as Jacob (vss. 1,2,34). But the two names are not simply doublets. They reflect a complex tradition about the third patriarch (cf. the discussion below). And no single source can lay exclusive claim to either line of the tradition. Moreover, in the Joseph story the two names interact within the scope of a single narration; the names point, not to disunity, but to a particular kind of structural unity characteristic for this story. In vss. 1–4 division of sources along the lines suggested by the two names would produce unnecessary fragmentation in a unit constructed along tight symmetrical lines. The same kind of argument would apply for the attempt to establish source distinctions between vss. 13 and 34 on the basis of the names. If one begins with the assumption that the chapter is unified, the names alone would not constitute sufficient basis to challenge the unity.[12]

Again in Gen 37, both Reuben (vss. 21,22,29) and Judah (vs. 26) try to prevent Joseph's murder. But there is no contradiction in their action, no doubling in the development of plot. Reuben first appeals to his brothers not to take Joseph's life, asking instead that the prey be confined in a well. Judah follows with a suggestion that Joseph be sold to the Ishmaelites. When that is done, Reuben returns to the well to find Joseph missing. His lamentation shows that he knew nothing of the sale. It does not contradict or double Judah's suggestion.[13] And no reason appears to me to argue that the story

---

Narratives, ed. Kenneth R. R. Gros Louis, James S. Ackerman, Thayer S. Warshaw (Nashville: Abingdon, 1974) 27.

[12] So, Rudolph, pp. 149–151. Cf. also the discussion below.

[13] So, Kessler, pp. 147–151.

cannot have two brothers working in different directions to preserve Joseph from murder.[14] Both actions belong together in the same line of narration. The same chapter multiplies explanations for the tense relationship between the brothers and Joseph as well as the nature of the brothers' response to Joseph's favored position. Thus, Joseph brings a bad report about the brothers to the father (vs. 2). Israel loves Joseph more than the others and gives him a special coat to demonstrate the favored position (vss. 3-4). Joseph recites his dreams, subordinating the brothers to his own position (vss. 5-11). And as a consequence, the brothers hate Joseph (vss. 4,8) and yet are jealous of him (vs. 11). But these variations are not self-contradictory, and they do not double the structure of the scene. To the contrary, they highlight intensifying emotions, a deeply set complex of problems within the scope of a single family.[15] Moreover, they contribute to the symmetrical structure of the exposition and, indeed, the entire chapter. To divide the chapter on the basis of such variations would split apart a marked symmetrical unity.

More difficult is the doublet involving the Ishmaelites (vss. 25,27,28, and Gen 39:1) and the Midianites (vss. 28,36). One must remember initially that the sentences in 37:36 and 39:1 are parallel, not by virtue of composition from pieces of two different sources, but rather by virtue of their function as pieces in a redactional device for incorporating ch. 38 into the total structure of the narration. Moreover, if one considers the reference to the Midianites in 37:28 as a gloss in the text, designed to attribute the disposition of Joseph by sale to the Ishmaelites to a third group rather than the brothers, the problem would look different.[16] The reference to the Midianites in vs. 28 would then be a doublet in *content* to 39:1 only *insofar as the gloss altered the primary form of the tradition* (cf. also 40:15; 42:22; 45:4). And the reference to the Midianites in 37:36, a redactional element as late in the tradition as the incorporation of ch. 38 into the narrative line, would be dependent on the gloss. The Midianite-Ishmaelite parallel would thus represent disunity in the text. But if this hypothesis has merit, the parallel would not point to two Joseph stories but to an expansion in the history of one story. If the disunity should then be attributed to E, would E not appear to be an expansion of a basic story rather than a doublet and parallel narration of that story?

A structural doublet in the exposition, vss. 1-4 in ch. 37, may also suggest an expansion of the basic story. Vs. 1 gives the exposition a firm beginning, a parallel with 47:27 at the end of the story. But the *toledoth* formula in vs. 2 also constitutes a beginning. Vss. 1-2 normally are attributed to P, with vss.

[14] Against Redford, pp. 132-135. Cf. the discussion below.
[15] Redford, p. 139, develops a significant reevaluation of this point.
[16] So, cf. Kessler, pp. 149-150.

3-4 the beginning exposition for the Yahwistic Joseph story. But this division does not solve the structural duplication between vss. 1 and 2. It seems more likely to me that the *toledoth* formula should be considered secondary in the opening movement of the story, an imitation of the opening formulas in the *Toledoth* book.[17] This formula might in some way be attributed to P, but not as evidence for a parallel P Joseph story. It would suggest more that a priestly expansion of the older Joseph story can be seen. Indeed, the formula sets the Joseph story into the larger context of traditions about Jacob and his sons. But beyond the formula, I can see nothing disruptive or redundant in the exposition. The remaining verses can be taken as a unified, symmetrical introduction. The structure analysis above would support this argument.[18]

The dream reports in vss. 5-11 constitute the next major element in the discussion of the source analysis. Critics commonly attribute all dream reports in the Joseph story to E.[19] But the only reason apparent in the discussion is that J does not normally have dream reports. The argument is not uncommon; yet, it suffers from the problems of circular reasoning by defining what J should look like and setting out the evidence accordingly. Since the dreams play a crucial role in the structure of the following verses, providing motivation for the brothers' radical disposal of Joseph, they must be taken together with at least vss. 19-20. The crucial question, then, concerns the unity of vss. 12-35. And various problems appear here.

Ruppert suggests cutting vss. 13b and 14a out of the initial conversation between Joseph and Jacob.[20] The apparent reason is that vs. 14a duplicates the commission in vs. 13a. Yet, the only indication of a duplication is the imperative form of the verb *hlk* in each speech. Nothing else in vs. 14a doubles vs. 13a. And no clear evidence for denying vs. 13b as a proper response to vs. 13a can be found. The text moves readily from Jacob speech to Joseph response to Jacob speech. The double imperative would stand, then, as a stylistic emphasis, not a doublet.[21] Ruppert also deletes vss. 15-18 from J, suggesting that the trip to Dothan here should be seen as a doublet of the trip to Shechem in J.[22] But the two trips cannot be defined simply as doublets. The Dothan stop functions structurally as a delay in the develop-

[17] Cf. Noth, p. 18, n. 53.

[18] Von Rad, *Genesis*, p. 350. Von Rad attributes all of vs. 2 to P since it mentions Joseph's tale-bearing as a source of the brothers' hatred, a motif not developed in the remaining parts of the scene. In addition, P should be the source interested in details like Joseph's age. There are difficulties in vs. 2. Why, for example, are the sons of Leah not mentioned? Yet, to eliminate that part of the verse following the *toledoth* formula from the substantial body of the scene seems unnecessarily arbitrary. Insofar as structure in the exposition is concerned, this part of vs. 2 fits well with vss. 3-4. Cf. the structural analysis above.

[19] Ruppert, pp. 30-35. For an effective critique of this position, cf. Redford, p. 69.

[20] Ruppert, p. 29.

[21] Cf. Rudolph, p. 153.

[22] Ruppert, pp. 29-30.

ment of tension focused on the Shechem destination. The same problem appears in the division of vs. 18 between J and E. The verse is crucial since it contains a change in scene. But to divide it seems totally unjustified. In both cases, the narration develops along a single line. Vss. 19–20 then follow vs. 18b so naturally that regardless of the source identification for vs. 18b, vss. 19–20 would necessarily be considered the same, a speech carrying the force of the narration in vs. 18b. And it is into this context that the dream reports of vss. 5–11 also fit.

A more pressing problem in the structure of this scene appears in vss. 21–24. Vss. 21–22 contain two distinct speeches, each with its own narrated introduction, each attributed to Reuben, each designed to forestall the plot to kill Joseph.[23] The only principal structural difference between the two speeches is that the first (vs. 21) employs a first person plural verb, the second a second person plural verb with 'al negation. To recognize two sources here would clarify the structure of the scene. But even with the Midianite—Ishmaelite doublet, this combination of speeches would constitute meager evidence for identifying a second *parallel* source in the chapter. A parallel E account here would seem to me to be hopelessly fragmented and highly hypothetical. One might respond by arguing that if vss. 22–24 were attributed to E, then vss. 29–35 might well follow in the same source since they depend on the plan to throw Joseph into one of the pits. But that would leave J without an account of Joseph's descent into Egypt. And J would certainly have had such an element. The only substantial evidence for compound sources in the chapter, then, lies in the double speech. One must remember, of course, that conclusions about this pattern remain tentative. Perhaps it reflects an expansion of the story like the one represented by the Midianite—Ishmaelite doublet. Perhaps it signals the fragments of a parallel source. But I would suggest, to the contrary, that a stylistic device in a single source narration of the scene may be present. *That device is to double speeches at the crucial turning points in the story's plot.*[24]

Moreover, vss. 23–24 connect readily with vs. 22 and should be attributed to the same source. Vss. 32aa and 32ab constitute stylistic doublets, not structural doublets. They should thus not be divided among different sources.[25] The entire chapter, with the exception of the *toledoth* formula, the

---

[23] Ruppert, p. 29, suggests changing Reuben in vs. 21 to Judah. The reason is that J is, according to definition, the source with Judah depicted as the helping brother. But if vs. 21 is changed to Judah, it would no longer be a clear doublet to vs. 22. For a critique of the position, cf. Speiser, *Genesis,* p. 291.

[24] Von Rad, *Genesis,* p. 350, observes: "It is not certain whether this doubleness is the trace of two sources. One could prefer to consider this complex motivation . . . as an indication of the successive, preliterary growth of the material in the Joseph story." Significantly, von Rad finds the Ishmaelite—Midianite parallel to be the only firm evidence of E in the chapter. But cf. my suggestion for dealing with this problem above.

[25] Against Ruppert, p. 30.

Midianite element in vs. 28a, and perhaps the Reuben speech in vs. 21, can be understood as the product of a single source, a scene in the story that is structurally sound and functionally unified. And even the two basic problems in unity in the chapter, the Midianite question and the doubled Reuben speech, may reflect a redactional method and the stylistic form of the primary source.[26] The question of sources here is crucial, since analysis in subsequent chapters depends on conclusions about this chapter. If one were to assume from the beginning that two sources are here, then he could parcel out the verses to those sources with some degree of confidence. If, however, one does not assume that two sources are present, if one assumes to the contrary that only one source is present and attempts to evaluate the evidence that might deny the assumption, then the parceling process is not so obvious. The strongest evidence *can be* understood *without* reference to J and E as parallel sources of the same story, the one simply inserted as fragments into the other.

These tentative conclusions can now be tested by reference to the remaining chapters in the Joseph story. Recent source critics have not contested the literary unity of either ch. 39 or ch. 40, with only minor exceptions in occasional verse fragments. In ch. 39 Ruppert eliminates only vs. 4a as a harmonizing gloss, an allusion to an E passage in 40:4.[27] From ch. 40 Ruppert eliminates vss. 3b,5b,15 as J elements since they allude to ch. 39, and the two chapters, he believes, derive from different sources.[28] In both chapters, incidentally, the necessity for identifying these verses as glosses would disappear should one conclude that the two chapters come from the same source. For Ruppert, ch. 39 is clearly J. But ch. 40 could not be J since it involves a dream report, and that kind of material should, according to the hypothesis, come from E.[29] But the argument begs the question. Structurally, the two chapters are interdependent. The unit in ch. 40 begins in 39:20b. 39:20b–23 and 40:1 seem clearly to be J in the opinion of most literary critics. The crucial question, then, concerns the remaining parts of ch. 40. Should it be removed from its J context and set aside as a different source?

It seems to me to be clear that the dream report in itself does not justify such a conclusion. There is, nonetheless, some difficulty in the transition from the one scene to the other (cf. the excursus above). The question, then, is whether that difficulty can be understood properly as evidence for parallel sources. Such a conclusion would assert that chs. 39 and 40 are essentially doublets of the same scene, each reporting the same events in its own particular way. But that conclusion I find difficult to sustain, as suggested by

[26] Cf. also Kessler, pp. 150–151.
[27] Ruppert, p. 44.
[28] Ruppert, p. 61; cf. also Noth, p. 38.
[29] Ruppert, p. 61.

the structural analysis. Fundamental in the narration of the digression is the picture of Joseph as an ideal administrator who lands in prison because of a false accusation. The one scene places Joseph in the role of ideal administrator who falls prey to a false accusation, while the other builds on Joseph as the dream interpreter *in prison,* not simply Joseph the servant. And the final scene in the digression presupposes both Joseph, the ideal administrator, and Joseph, the dream interpreter in prison. It would seem to me to be a better course of procedure, then, to attribute the difficulty in transition to the growth of the story from various oral sources rather than to the combination of two literary sources.

Ch. 41, moreover, follows from ch. 40 without a break. Ruppert notes that vss. 1–24 depend on ch. 40, with the exception of vs. 14a.[30] Vs. 14a he attributes to J since it alludes to 39:20–23. If, however, ch. 40 should be J, all of 41:1–12 could be attributed to J without breaking its unified structure. And if the dream reports are not denied categorically to J, vss. 25–29 could also be attributed to J. Indeed, these verses obviously follow from vss. 1–7. Regardless of the source designation, chs. 40 and 41:1–29 would seem clearly to belong to the same source.

Apparent contradictions and repetitions appear in the remaining verses of the scene.[31] The famine infects Egypt (vss. 30a,55a), and the whole land (vss. 30b–31,54b). Joseph recommends that the Pharaoh find one man to head the grain works (vss. 33,34b) and that several men should be appointed to gather the grain (vss. 34a,35). In vs. 34 a fifth of the harvest in the land should be stored, in vs. 35 the entire harvest. Joseph's inspection appears in vs. 46 and again in vss. 47–48. Vs. 48 uses *'ōkel* for the food gathered, while vs. 49 uses *bār.* And the famine itself is reported in vs. 54 and again in vs. 55. But the most important of the duplications in this section of the scene is in a series of Pharaoh speeches appointing Joseph to high office. The two speeches in succession, vss. 39–40 do not, in fact, duplicate each other, the one elevating Joseph to a position over the Pharaoh's house and the other placing him over all the land of Egypt. But the third speech, vs. 41, duplicates the second.

Yet, all of these repetitions belong essentially to the same category of stylistic patterns noted above. The point is especially clear in the report of Joseph's inspection in vss. 46–48. The first stage in this report, vs. 46, functions as a general statement of Joseph's activity: "Joseph went out from the Pharaoh and passed through all the land of Egypt." The second part describes the specific purpose of the work: "During the seven years of fertility, the land produced abundantly. He gathered all the food during the

---

[30] Ruppert, p. 68.
[31] For an analysis of these contradictions and repetitions as criteria for making source distinctions, cf. Ruppert, p. 68–69. Cf. also von Rad, *Genesis,* p. 372.

seven years (or, with LXX: during those seven years the fertility continued) in the land of Egypt." The shift in vocabulary between vss. 48 and 49 does not point to any greater division. The term, '*ōkel,* is general; *bār* is specific. The same kind of observation applies for the report of the famine in vss. 54–55. The verses do not duplicate each other. They constitute one statement about the famine, moving from a general observation to a specific one: "There was famine in all lands. But in the land of Egypt there was bread. When all the land of Egypt was famished, the people cried to the Pharaoh for bread." Then follows an account of the procedure for obtaining food. Moreover, the designation of famine in Egypt and famine in the whole land, the parallel between vss. 30 and 31 or vss. 54 and 55, is no contradiction but rather intensification. The famine hits both Egypt and the whole land.

The one problematic text, perhaps the one clear doublet, in the series lies in vss. 39–41 and 44. Two distinct Pharaoh speeches, separated only by a brief narration, elevate Joseph to office. Yet, even here the speeches do not constitute sufficient evidence for a definition of parallel sources. To the contrary, here as in the Reuben speeches in ch. 37, the doubling characteristic may represent a particular stylistic device in the Joseph story, employed at crucial turning points in the story's plot. Moreover, I can see no conflict between Joseph's office and several officials appointed to carry out his work (vss. 33–35). The process involves a complex office; thus, the text piles up descriptions of the work in the office. The entire digression, then, appears to me to be unified, at least insofar as analysis for parallel sources is concerned. Even vss. 46a and 51–52, regularly attributed to P since P likes to include such items of information, need not be denied out of hand to the unit, for they do not violate the structure of the whole. If these verses are P, they would represent expansions of the basic narration rather than evidence for an independent, parallel source.

In the next scene of the story, the complication of tension in ch. 42, similar repetitions appear. One brother finds money in his food bag along the way (vss. 27–28) before all the brothers find money in their bags when they return home (vs. 35). It is possible, to be sure, to define this curiosity in the text as evidence of a doublet; yet, as suggested in the structural analysis above, such a conclusion cannot be considered a necessity. Moreover, the scene reports twice that the brothers arrived in Egypt. Twice it notes that Joseph recognized them (vss. 5–8). And it raises two distinct speeches of accusation against the brothers (vss. 9 and 14). But to divide these repetitions into distinct sources damages the artistic composition of the scene.[32]

Von Rad goes one step farther: "A much more profound inconsistency appears in the continuation of the narrative in ch. 43:1ff. There every reader

---

[32] Cf. Rudolph, p. 160. Cf. the discussion of these problems, particularly the money problem, in the structural analysis above.

must notice that the brothers did not go back to Egypt at once, as one would expect them to do, to redeem the imprisoned Simeon, but that they remained quietly in the land until their supply of grain finally was consumed and their need forced them to a second buying trip."[33] The inconsistency is clearly there. But it is an exegetical problem, not a literary-critical one. The inconsistency belongs to the brothers as they are depicted by the story, or perhaps to Jacob, but not to the text. Indeed, it is just this inconsistency that demonstrates contrary to von Rad's position that the brothers' character had not changed from the time they sold Joseph into slavery. The story reports no strong objection against the delays for the sake of Simeon. To the contrary, the brothers were willing to leave Simeon in prison, just as they were willing to leave Joseph to his fate. And while that action is inconsistent with standards commonly expected to govern relationships among brothers, it is not inconsistent with the characterization of *these* brothers. The chapter is again unified. It shows no basic disharmony with its context. It shows no structural breaks, no doublets.

The first part of the next scene offers no problem for source analysis. Gen 43–44 belongs entirely to J. But the crucial ending for the scene, the element that carries the full denouement of the story, in ch. 45, is problematic. Twice Joseph announces his identity to his brothers (vss 3–4). Twice he requests them to bring the father to Egypt (vss. 9,13). Joseph requires his Egyptian servants to leave the room (vs. 1), yet he cries so loudly that all can hear (vss. 2,16). In contrast to Joseph's invitation to his father and brothers to settle in Goshen (vss. 9–10), the Pharaoh invites them to settle in the best of Egypt's land (vss. 18–20). He sends wagons (vss. 19,27) or perhaps only laden animals (vs. 17) or perhaps Joseph provided the animals (vs. 23). Yet, again the plurality in the chapter lends itself to artistic structure in a single source but not to convincing evidence for distinguishing two parallel sources.[34] None of the pairs can be defined as self-contradictory or even real doublets. In each case stylistic intensification heightens the effect of the scene, like the doulbe dream reports in Gen 37 and 40–41. And the double self-revelation speech from Joseph to his brothers fits the same pattern for duplicating speeches noted above. The denouement in Gen 43–45 thus appears to me to be unified. As in the rest of the story, it would not show evidence of composition from two parallel sources.

The theophany report in Gen 46:1b–5a conflicts with the context provided by the itinerary in vs. 1a; these verses set out a divine command for Jacob's journey after Jacob himself had already decided to go. Moreover, the report connects with patriarchal traditions about Beer-sheba. It is not surprising, then, that the unit has been generally attributed to E. Indeed, Odil Steck

---

[33] Von Rad, *Genesis,* p. 381.
[34] Rudolph, p. 163–164.

suggests that in these verses the entire scope of the Elohistic bridge between patriarchs and exodus can be seen.[35] Ruppert notes to the contrary that the point of contact here is Gen 26:1-5, a passage from J.[36] Why he then labels the unit E_2 seems at best unclear. If nevertheless Steck's suggestion should prove decisive, then a valuable insight into the structure of E would have been established.

The impact of the insight, however, is not immediately obvious. Would it mean that E has no fully developed Joseph story? Or is the theophany report perhaps dependent on the larger redactional context in Gen 37-50, particularly on the account of Jacob's death? Moreover, the position of the report in the Joseph story interprets the story as a whole as a bridge and makes particular contact with the image of Jacob descending into Egypt to Joseph. Can the report, then, not be understood as an extension of the larger story context, a commentary on its significance? Would that role, moreover, not offer a distinctive insight into the character of E?

The itinerary in vss. 1a and 5-6 enframes the theophany report and the following name list. The name list, vss. 8-24, may well derive from P or a secondary redactional element in P. The remaining part of the chapter and 47:1-6 belong clearly to J. Vss. 7-11 have been assigned to P because of the stiff and solemn style, particularly the emphasis on the number of years in Jacob's sojourn.[37] Yet, this concluding conversation between the Pharaoh and Jacob is not out of place in the development of J. And a fragment of P here does not fit into other evidence for a P Joseph story. It may be P, perhaps a secondary redactional element in P. But the text is nevertheless remarkably well unified. Vs. 12, along with vss. 13-26, belongs to J. Vs. 27a brings the basic narration of the story to its conclusion, also a part of J. Vs. 27b would derive from P (cf. Ex 1:7).

Evidence to support the hypothesis that E runs a parallel story alongside J and that the two have been combined into a single, artistic whole thus appears to me to be very thin. P may have expanded the Joseph story by occasional commentary and by extensive additions, like 47:7-26. But there is no evidence for a parallel P Joseph story. This point would provoke no objections. But does the same point not also apply to E? If one can indeed speak of E in the Joseph story, can he do more than demonstrate a theological and traditional expansion of the Yahwistic story? The entire story demonstrates a basic structural and functional unity, with perhaps the exception of the theological expansions. Indeed, it fulfills a crucial theological and structural function for the Yahwist. It sets the stage for the fulfillment of God's promise to the patriarchs and Israel's exodus from

---

[35] Steck, p. 121 in n. 291.
[36] Ruppert, pp. 130-132.
[37] Von Rad, Genesis, p. 407. Noth, p. 38, assigns these verses to E.

Egypt. And it fits the character of the Yahwist's kerygma by emphasizing the blessing Jacob brings for the Pharaoh when he enters the land of Egypt.[38]

B. *Second edition hypotheses.* Redford makes a new proposal about the literary history of the Joseph story.[39] He agrees with Whybray that no clear evidence for dividing the story between two parallel sources, between J and E, can be found. But his conclusions are quite the opposite of the ones defended by Whybray. His concern is not to argue for the unity of the story but to suggest that the two sources, which he finds in the Joseph story just as the classical source critics suggested, are not contiguous with the Elohistic and Yahwistic sources in the rest of the Pentateuch. Rather, he finds a basic edition of the story, one that uses the names Reuben and Jacob, and a subsequent edition, an inferior manipulation of the story that emphasizes Judah and Israel. The former, as Redford notes, is equivalent to the source which critics have traditionally labelled E, the latter to the source normally identified as J.

Redford begins a defense of the hypothesis with an analysis of Gen 37. An initial step is to isolate two distinct roles, doublets in character, for a "good" brother. The Reuben role has moral and literary superiority over the Judah role. The Reuben source is thus morally and literarily superior to the Judah expansion. Moreover, he observes that in those cases where Reuben appears in the dominant position, the name for the father is normally Jacob. In the texts with Judah in the leading role, the father is normally Israel.

Redford's description of the evidence is in itself impressive and presents a strong case. But is the description an accurate one? Will it support the weight of his argument? The development of the case depends first on the assertion that a good story could not have two "good" brothers. That two distinct roles for the two "good" brothers appear is clear. It may even be possible, though a little cavalier, to conclude that Reuben acts in a manner that is morally superior to Judah's acts. But this observation does not prove that two literary levels can be identified from the two roles. The roles are not doublets. Indeed, I can see no good reasons for concluding that the Judah role is an expansion of an original, morally superior role for Reuben. The two roles present different activity on the part of two distinct principals in the plot. Redford asserts that the story could not have two brothers doing the same thing since to do so would incomprehensibly weaken the sub-plot. But he offers no evidence to support the assertion. The two brothers do not do the same thing, as Redford's observation about the morally superior role of Reuben would suggest. To the contrary, they add to the tension of the plot by their contrast.

---

[38] Wolff, p. 157, refers to vss, 13–26 in evaluating the role of the Joseph story in the kerygma of the Yahwist. But it is obvious that 47:7–10 functions more directly to this end. This text has normally been attributed to P (or E) and thus arbitrarily eliminated from Wolff's attention.

[39] Redford, pp. 106–186.

Moreover, the argument from the name patterns draws from evidence that is equivocal in character. The pattern appears, not so much within the speeches of Judah and Reuben, speeches that would show their leading roles (the only exception is 43:8), but rather larger contexts. In ch. 42 Jacob and Reuben appear together with no reference to Israel or Judah. In ch. 43 the names shift to Israel and Judah with no reference to Jacob and Reuben. Given the hypothesis that two sources or two editions appear here, the evidence can be organized to fit the divisions. But if one assumes that the story might not be so divided, then the evidence does not appear so convincing, at least not convincing enough to substantiate a *prima facie* case.[40]

But is that assumption justified? If it is, then some other explanation for the alternation between the names must be forthcoming. The crucial issue lies in the shift between the names "Jacob" and "Israel." These names are clearly doublets, while the Reuben/Judah parallel constitutes a similar phenomenon only if one accepts the assertion that the story could not have two distinct brothers in similar roles. If my argument that chs. 42 and 43 cannot be parcelled out to two sources or editions should have any merit, is there an explanation that would account for the shift between the names "Jacob" and "Israel?" The crucial element in the pattern is the appearances of the name "Israel" since "Jacob" is used more widely throughout the story. Excluding for the moment the stereotyped formula, *bᵉnê-yiśrā'ēl*, the name appears in 37:3,13; 43:6,8,11; 45:28; 46:1,29,30; and 47:27. In these verses, the *immediate narrative* context, not just the large inclusive context of a scene, does not focus on a relationship between Israel and Judah. The one exception to the observation is 43:8. But even in 43:8 Judah's speech addressed to his father Israel does not place the weight of content on a dominant role for Judah. To the contrary, the concern here centers on the shift of a principal in the story from Canaan to Egypt, in this case, Benjamin.

The same point can be made for all of the other occurrences of the name. In ch. 37, vs. 3 shows Israel as the father who loved Joseph more than all the others and gave that beloved son a special coat to symbolize his love. That verse is a part of the exposition, introducing the name Israel into the flow of the narrative. But in addition, that introduction provides a motif that motivates the brothers' treachery and is thus fundamental for the account of Joseph's move to Egypt. Moreover, in vs. 13 Israel commissions Joseph, who wears his coat of fatherly love, for the trip that eventually led him to Egypt. In ch. 43, the three appearances of the name involve the father Israel in a similar shift from Canaan to Egypt, with a second favorite son at stake. In vs. 8 Judah's speech places Judah in a leading role. But the narration context does not focus on that role. It focuses on the fateful necessity for

[40] As does Redford, p. 135.

Benjamin to go to Egypt, following Joseph into certain danger. And the exchange concludes in vs. 11, as in 37:13, with a commission that sends a beloved son on a journey that ends in Egypt. Finally, in 45:28, another shift from Canaan to Egypt dominates the narrative. Israel, the father of Joseph, announces that he too will go to Egypt in order to see his son. In ch. 46, vss. 29–30 complete the shift. Joseph meets Israel in Goshen and Israel addresses his long-lost son. The name, "Israel," thus appears specifically in those texts concerned with the move to Egypt, first of Joseph, then of Benjamin, and finally of the father himself. Moreover, the two formula occurrences, 42:5 and 45:21, involve the stereotyped $b^e n\hat{e}$-$yi\acute{s}r\bar{a}'\bar{e}l$ in the shift from Canaan to Egypt as well.

My principal point is to suggest that the appearance of the name Israel is not to be understood in isolation from the name Jacob as evidence of a literary stratum, supported by the primary role of Judah. The pattern of its appearance does not point to divisions within the story but to emphasis on crucial points of the story. But can the thesis not be expanded a step? Why should the author use a shift in names for the father to emphasize the shift from Canaan to Egypt? The answer to that question is to be found, perhaps, in the concern of the story to account for not only a shift from Canaan to Egypt but also the shift from the patriarch Jacob to the people Israel. The parallel established by the opening and closing sentences of the story, Jacob in Canaan, Israel in Egypt, would suggest that concern. Moreover, in two of the three pericopes in Genesis where the names Jacob and Israel appear together, Gen 32:23–33 and 35:9–15, the combination does not point to two. literary strata within the pericope but to a tradition concerned to account for the shift from the patriarch Jacob to the patriarch Israel. The thesis must remain hypothetical. Yet, it does suggest that the Jacob/Israel parallel has a tradition history that cannot be resolved simply in terms of literary strata, as if J should possess one name and E the other. Moreover, an argument from the combination of names, Reuben and Jacob or Judah and Israel, mixes evidence from two different kinds of phenomena. Rueben and Judah play two distinct and opposing roles. Jacob and Israel are names for one principal. To force both into a single pattern is an unnecessarily contrived procedure. The evidence from these points seems to me to be unconvincing.[41]

Judah's counsel, vss. 26–27, builds its structure, so Redford suggests, as an imitation of Reuben's counsel, vs. 22.[42] The observation may well be correct. Yet, it does not argue for a later edition in the story, but for a second speech in the narrative patterned for parallel and contrast on the basis of the first speech. The pit motif is also an indication of the secondary character of the

---

[41] Cf. Rudolph's evaluation of the name game, pp. 148–151.
[42] Redford, p. 140.

Judah version, according to Redford. In the Reuben version, the pit is central, a means for confining Joseph until the "good" brother can return to rescue him. In the Judah version, however, the pit is a needless vestige of the Reuben edition. Judah suggests taking Joseph out of the pit to sell him. But the needless character of the pit motif is apparent only if the Judah version has already been siphoned away from its counterpart. If one assumes from the beginning that the plot might be unified, the extraneous character of the pit might not be so obvious.

Thus, the evidence does not support a hypothesis that defines two extensive editions of the Joseph story. There is some justification for concluding that the Joseph story now appears in an expanded edition. The position of Gen 38 and 47:28–50:14 would confirm this observation, and the theological expansions noted above would round out the picture. But the evidence does not support an isolation of a second edition of the story along the lines proposed by Redford.

The more pressing problem lies in Redford's denial of continuity between the Joseph story and the rest of the Pentateuch.[43] This problem is not only a matter of structural context, but also a question of source identity. Does the Joseph story have any role to play in the Yahwistic source, a source that includes the patriarchal stories and the exodus traditions? Redford develops five observations:

1) He avers that the story shows marked traces of single, rather than composite authorship. This point I would affirm. Indeed, I would want to argue for a more thorough-going unity of composition than does Redford. But unity of authorship in the Joseph story says nothing about the connections the story might have with the patriarchal and exodus traditions. Nor does it say anything about the story's affinities with the Yahwistic source. J contains stories of various genres, with varying histories of growth. Unity of authorship in one story, even if it is a long one, does not deny that J may have used it. It does not mean that the Yahwist created it. It would suggest only that the Yahwist incorporated an independent story into the structure of his narration.

2) Redford also argues that the Joseph story has no interest in pseudo-historical explanation or cult topography, as the patriarchal stories do. But the point is not that the Joseph story shows genre or intention patterns in common or at variance with the patriarchal stories. There is no doubt that the Joseph story is different from the patriarchal stories in both structure and genre. But even in the patriarchal stories, not every unit has the same kind of interest in historical, topological, or cultic explanation. Various kinds of tradition can appear together in the composition of a single source.

3) The theological outlook of Gen 37–50, according to Redford, is

different from the patriarchal narrations. The point is again well taken. There is a theological subtlety in the Joseph story which cannot be found in the patriarchal narration. Yet, one must not push the point too far. Redford maintains that no reference to covenant or promise appears here, no theophany to interrupt the course of events and tax the imagination of the twentieth-century reader. Gen 46:1-5 has, of course, been eliminated from consideration. Yet, it seems to me that it is not so easy to deny the concern for Jacob's posterity, reflected especially in 45:4-13, but overarching the entire scope of the story. Moreover, it is difficult to ignore the structural dialectic of the story. That dialectic is not peripheral to the story. It is the very basis of the plot.

4) The Joseph story does not show the religious and racial exclusiveness of the patriarchal stories. This point is again significant. But the issue is not whether the Joseph story has an identical point of view with the patriarchal stories, stories stamped by a long process of oral transmission. It is quite clear that it does not. The issue is whether there is any continuity with the patriarchal stories, any role to play in bringing the patriarchal stories to completion and opening the exodus narration.

5) In a final statement, Redford concludes that the immediate context of the patriarchal and exodus narratives does not provide any points to dovetail with the Joseph story; the tradition history of Israel's early period has nothing in common with the Joseph narration. But again, the question cannot demand uniformity in the history of the tradition. That the brothers cower in the Joseph story but not, for example, in Gen 34 is irrelevant to the question. There is no evidence that Rachel is still living in the Joseph story if one takes the allusion to the mother in the dream as a necessity dictated by the astral imagery. The mother would provide only a possibility for contact with the double figures suggested by the sun and the moon without playing a substantial role in the plot. And finally, the questions of tribal history are irrelevant to the issue. One patriarchal story may have an interest in tribal history, another may not. There is no doubt that the Joseph story is not like the patriarchal stories. But that unique character does not mean that it has no contact with the patriarchal or exodus traditions and no contact with J.

Perhaps the most important argument, however, is that the Joseph story fits well into the theology of the Yahwist.[44] Jacob arrives in Goshen, and at the same time offers blessing to the Pharaoh. Without speaking specifically to the theological interest of the Yahwist, to the structural patterns of the

---

[44] My concern here is not so much to argue from date to continuity or discontinuity with the Yahwist. Cf. John van Seters, "Confessional Reformulation of the Exilic Period in the Pentateuch," *VT* (1972) 448-459, where he suggests a significantly later date for the Yahwist than the one normally designated. My concern here is to argue that the Joseph story has a structural and theological consistency with the Yahwist. Cf. Wolff, p. 157. Some attention for the question of date will be registered below.

Yahwistic source with its heavy dependency on the Joseph story as a transition from the patriarchs to the exodus, one cannot dismiss the continuity of the Joseph story with its context.[45]

Thus, it seems to me to be clear that the Joseph story must be understood essentially as a unit, an artistic masterpiece. But the masterpiece does not appear to me to be a product of a redactor who expressed his art by weaving together two originally distinct sources. Nor does the masterpiece appear to me to have been compromised by a later, clumsy hand. The masterpiece remains masterpiece as it now stands, each piece in its place. Rhythm, symmetry, harmony, heightened on occasion by contrasts, contribute to the flow of this ancient literary symphony.

III. ORAL SOURCES AND TRADITION HISTORY

Before conclusions can be set out about the origin of the story and its relationship to the Yahwist, however, one final set of questions must be considered. What kind of tradition history can be reconstructed that might clarify the origin of this narrative. Two substantial contributions to the discussion of tradition history in the Joseph story facilitate a brief review of this facet in the evaluation. Hannelis Schulte traces the history of the Joseph story through four oral stages, as well as two written ones. The earliest stage would have involved a tale about unnamed brothers who sold their youngest sibling into slavery, only later to travel to Egypt because of famine and stand before an unrecognized, powerful official. The youngest brother, now an official of power, recognized them, accused them falsely (three variants of the accusation appear here), and imprisoned them. Then follow the reunion, the gifts, and the trip home. The second stage attaches the tale to Jacob and five sons (Reuben, Simeon, Levi, Judah, and Joseph). The third stage would have introduced Benjamin and a second trip to Egypt. The fourth stage then adds the blessing for Ephraim and Manasseh. The first literary stage ties the story to the larger traditions of Israel by raising the number of brothers to twelve and introducing the story of Joseph's rise to power in Egypt. (Are we to conclude that stage one has the brothers stand before a mysterious figure with no explanation for the manner of events that brought the youngest brother to that position?) This stage would contain the first reference to Jacob's shift from Canaan to Egypt (also the removal of his body back to Canaan). The final stage rounds out the narrative with finishing details such as the sale of Joseph to the prison master, the dreams, and various harmonizing points.[46]

Some such basic, traditional story about brothers who sold their youngest

---

[45] I do not want to argue that the Yahwist was the author of the Joseph story. On the relationship between the author and the Yahwist, cf. the comments below.

[46] Schulte, pp. 27–28.

sibling, only to meet him later as a figure of power in a foreign country, may lie behind the Joseph story. And that traditional tale may have been essentially a story of flight to Egypt in the face of famine, like Gen 12:10–20. Yet, must we not ask carefully whether that kind of hypothetical, oral stage would constitute a stage in the tradition history of the Joseph story or an *oral source,* used by the author of the Joseph story in the construction of his own, original narrative. The hypothetical character of the oral stages is problem enough. But even if one could control the hypothetical first stage, would that stage lay any claim to identity as *Joseph* story? Or would it have been nothing more for the author of the story than the traditional legend of Hamlet was for Shakespeare? Even in the second and third stages, should these distinctions stand critical evaluation, would a story about Jacob and five sons making a simple trip or two in order to stave off starvation count as an oral stage, a *Vorform* in the history of the Joseph story? The question is important when one asks whether these oral stages in the history of the Joseph story functioned in any manner as a transition between patriarchs and exodus. Schulte's reconstruction disallows such a conclusion. But with that position, it would seem to me to be necessary to insist that oral stages like these could lay no claim for identity as original forms of the Joseph story but only as oral sources, transformed radically by the literary production at Schulte's stage five.[47] If that should be the case, however, then Schulte's dismissal of Noth's position regarding the Joseph story would be unjustified. She argues: "Steht aber diese Vorform der Geschichte fest, so wird M. Noths Ansicht hinfällig, dass die Joseph Geschichte aus dem Satz entstanden sei, 'Jakob und seine Söhne zogen nach Ägypten herab.'"[48] But the argument would depend on establishing the oral levels as *Vorformen* of the Joseph story as such. And that conclusion does not seem to me to be justified.

Yet, even in the face of such a caveat as that, Schulte's reconstruction may prove quite helpful. It would suggest that certain formulations, problematic in the literary unity of the Joseph story, formulations such as variants in the accusation against the brothers, could be understood from traditional formulations in the oral sources. This point is most relevant in evaluating the unity of the digression. Moreover, it points to problems in weighing the narrative for evidence of two parallel literary sources, for in this reconstruction, stage five is the productive literary stage, with stage six at best an expansion of the previous level.[49] Is one to conclude that stage five was really

---

[47] One might still ask whether a traditional story could be transformed so completely without leaving more extensive evidence of its character as oral tradition somewhere within the Jacob cycle. That may well be possible in principle. But what basis then exists for defining the character of the oral stage? Is the reconstruction too hypothetical to be helpful in understanding the origin of the Joseph story?

[48] Schulte, p. 26.

[49] So, Schulte, pp. 14–19.

a dual stage, with two literary artisans transforming the oral sources into two parallel, distinct, but obviously related stories? Or is the second literary source, traditionally identified as the Elohist, to be seen as anything more than Schulte's stage six? It is, incidentally, clear from the tradition history outlined here that the creative moment in the production of the Joseph story is a literary one. In structure, as well as genre, the Joseph story belongs to the production of the artist's hand at a literary level rather than the production of the folk at an oral level.[50]

Less hypothetical and more helpful in evaluating the tradition history of the Joseph story is the analysis by W. Lee Humphreys. Humphreys concentrates primarily on the role of the wise courtier in the Joseph story, thus opening his work with an examination of chs. 39–41.[51] The story in Gen 39–41 would represent a distinct kernel for Humphreys, an independent story borrowed by the author of the Joseph story to account for Joseph's rise to power once he had arrived in Egypt. As a part of the Joseph story, it would be a fully integrated scene in the plot. "It is the goal of Gen 37, and the assumed format upon which Gen 42ff depends (cf. Gen 45:4–8), and the basis upon which it works to a resolution."[52] Yet, the story maintains its own integrity. "On the other hand, the story of Joseph in Egypt does not show such dependence on its companion piece. The tensions of (39) 40–41 are created and fully resolved by the end of chapter 41. . . ."[53] This conclusion can be supported by genre analysis, a step that shows 39–41 to be a *legend* with its own distinct intention, appropriated as a scene within a larger *novella* without violation of its own internal unity.[54]

Humphreys argues, moreover, for an isolation of ch. 39 within the kernel story. A distinction between chs. 39 and 40 may well be warrented in a discussion of the legend's tradition history. As a traditional legend the story as it now stands in chs. 39–41 would have grown over the course of oral transmission, open to incorporation of a motif similar to the Egyptian *Story of the Two Brothers,* or perhaps a motif about dreams in a prison. But in such a traditional legend, it can be a mistake to attribute stages to literary, parallel sources. The distinctions here derive, at best, from complexities in the tradition's history, not from combinations in literary composition. That observation, however, does not deny Schulte's contention that the Egyptian story itself was included in the Joseph story at the point of its literary production. The observation points simply to the oral character of the Egyptian story, as well as the literary production of the Joseph story *qua* Joseph story.

[50]So, Coats, "The Joseph Story . . . ," pp. 295–296.

[51] Humphreys, pp. 205–208; see note 59 below.

[52] Humphreys, p. 207.

[53] Humphreys, p. 207.

[54] Coats, "The Joseph Story . . . ," pp. 288–291.

Humphreys develops an interpretation of tradition history that would show the significance of the wise courtier model from chs. (39) 40–41 for the tale of the brothers in Egypt. Under normal circumstances the motif depends on the relationship between the wise courtier and the king. But in chs. 42ff that focal relationship is broken. Now the story develops around the relationship between the wise courtier and his own particular family. And it is through the focus on the family that the unique theological interests of the Joseph story can be seen. That position I would affirm.[55]

Yet, the questions about unity between chs. 39 and 40 remain a problem. Humphreys suggests that ch. 39 may have been incorporated into the legend by the Yahwist at this creative stage for the Joseph story as a whole, rather than in the tradition history of the story about Joseph in Egypt. The problem is that while some distinction between chs. 39 and 40 may be detected, suggesting development in the story's history, the intention of ch. 39 more nearly facilitates the concerns of the legend about the wise courtier in the stages of his rise to the Pharaoh's court than the concerns of the Joseph story as a whole. The evidence to the contrary is the reference to the divine assistance for Joseph in ch. 39. But the use of that formula is not at all the same as the divine guidance motif in ch. 45. The divine assistance formulas in ch. 39 facilitate Joseph's wise and successful administration of his office, not divine guidance of events toward a particular goal despite human involvement.

In any case, it is clear from an analysis of tradition history that the antecedents of the Joseph story did not serve a transition function. That function comes only with the expansion of the story to its full flower. But in its full flower, it roots its transition function, not in external elements of the story, but in the intrinsic dialectic of the story's plot. It is significant, then, that the prior stages in the history of the Joseph story, represented by the legend of the wise courtier, do not center on the movement from Canaan to Egypt. A story about temporary movement from Canaan to Egypt as a means for meeting the crisis of a famine seems too hypothetical to provide significant insight into the origin of the Joseph story. But even if one should grant the plausibility of such a story, the movement would not be its focus. There would have been no transition role, but, like Gen 12:10–20, only a story about a movement to meet a crisis. The conclusion facilitated by these observations, however, is not that the Joseph story came to serve a transition function secondarily. To the contrary, the transition is fundamental for the narration of the story. The conclusion would be that the Joseph story was created from the beginning to serve such a function, to deal theologically and artistically with the transition from patriarchs to exodus. And that stage

---

[55] Coats, "The Joseph Story . . . ," pp. 293–297. Although my concern in that essay was different from the focus of Humphreys on the wise courtier, our conclusions are remarkably similar and tend to confirm the direction of interpretation.

of creativity is very close to the stage preserved in the received text. The story as it now appears is essentially unitary in character, with its sources not to be defined as *Vorformen,* much less parallel strands of the same story, but as oral stories or motifs used by the author to construct his narrative.

One final question, then, is in order. If the Joseph story is the product of a literary artisan, when and under what circumstances did he do his work? A classical position suggests that the story was produced in the Solomonic or post-Solomonic era, under the influence of wisdom circles, perhaps in the context of the royal court. Von Rad observed: "The Joseph story . . . is obviously related to the older teachings of wisdom. In fact, it has been thought that one can detect in the Joseph story joy in the opening of a larger horizon. . . . This awakened interest in the exotic is the sign of an age mature and enlightened, intellectually and culturally. And Solomon's era must be characterized as just that."[56] Redford denies such an early provenance. Part of the denial stems from his rejection of von Rad's thesis about wisdom influence in the story. And certainly it is correct to deny that the Joseph story is simply a wisdom story. But to make such a denial is not to undercut the elements of wisdom in the story.[57] But the denial also stems from Redford's evaluation of historical evidence. "All evidence examined above, on the other hand, both Biblical and extra-Biblical, clearly favours a date between the mid-seventh and mid-fifth centuries B.C. . . ."[58] Yet, more recently, Humphreys has challenged Redford's conclusions. He responds to Redford in terms of evidence cast into three categories: 1) Egyptian coloring of the narrative; 2) the supposed affinities with other tales which appear only in the latter part of the first millennium B.C.; and 3) words or phrases in the narrative characteristic of late Hebrew or Aramaic. His position is detailed throughout his manuscript on the Joseph story. But the specific responses to these three areas suggest the difficulty in accepting Redford's conclusion:

."It must be asked whether the so-called Egyptian coloring is a trustworthy guide, not only in the face of gaps in our knowledge of Egypt, especially in the first part of the first millennium B.C., but also given Redford's own judgement, with which this study agrees, that the author does not seem to be as well informed about things Egyptian as is often supposed. Can the work of one writing about Egypt from some distance and with some awe and wonder be pressed to the extent that Redford attempts? We have above suggested that there are affinities between the tale of Joseph in Egypt and such a tale as that dealing with the adventures of Sinuhe and with elements of the tomb biographies, and thus that one need not seek as late as Redford for related materials. Finally,

---

[56] Von Rad, *Genesis,* p. 435.
[57] So, Coats,."The Joseph Story . . . ," p. 296.
[58] Redford, p. 252.

vocabulary usage is a difficult criterion to apply, and the possibility that variations reflect, not only different periods in time, but circles of interest and tradition, different places of origin must be given more consideration than it usually is." [59]

With Humphreys' critique in mind, I do not see adequate evidence for denying von Rad's position. The Joseph story would appear to me to be the artistic creation of a literary master, a novella incorporating elements from various sources for a creation of his own insight.[60] And that work would have been harmonious with the creativity of the royal court in the Solomonic era. There is no evidence, unfortunately, to clarify the relationship between that master and the Yahwist. No evidence suggests that the Yahwist himself created the story for a structural transition in his larger work. He may have employed a story already created for theological purposes because that story also suited his own literary construct. But insofar as I can see, there is also no evidence to deny the possibility that the Yahwist himself was the artist who created the story. The question remains moot.

One might also raise a question about date and origin for the various expansions of the story. These elements are essentially too fragmentary to permit a firm conclusion. A clear definition of their character would depend on determining whether they reveal evidence of relationships with any other such expansion in the Pentateuch.

[59] W. Lee Humphreys, *The Joseph Narrative of Genesis, A Traditio-Historical Study,* an unpublished manuscript used here with the permission of the author; pp. 217–218.
[60] So, Coats, "The Joseph Story . . . ," p. 296.

CHAPTER 3

RECONCILIATION AND POLITICAL POWER

The Joseph story is a masterpiece of ancient literary genius. There is little room for doubt about such a conclusion. As a masterpiece, moreover, the story possesses universal elements of appeal. The purpose of this chapter is to elaborate three points from the story that may reflect such broader areas of appeal. These points were discussed briefly in the context of the structural analysis of chapter I. Now my concern is to pull that facet of the discussion together for more extensive exploration.

I. RECONCILIATION

Claus Westermann demonstrated that the principal scope of tension in the plot of the Joseph story centers in family relationships. [1] When the group of brothers sold Joseph to an unknown fate, the family suffered a break as permanent as death (cf. Gen 37:31–35). For the brothers and the father, hope for reconciliation was pointless. For Joseph it was beyond immediate realization. How can a family broken apart by treachery ever be reunited? Yet, the tension in the plot of the story builds precisely on that family's prospects for reconciliation. And the arch of tension develops in the interaction between the brothers (represented now by Reuben, now by Judah), the father, and Joseph.

If one searches the narration for some indication of guilt among the parties involved in the break, he surprisingly discovers that *all* principals share the taint of responsibility. The following paragraphs are designed to demonstrate that point.

A. The group of brothers bears an obvious guilt. From the opening lines of the story, the brothers are jealous, filled with hatred. It is thus not surprising that they plot to murder the object of their hate. Their murder plans do not succeed, because first Reuben, then Judah intercede at just the right point. But the alternative fate, at least in the brothers' eyes, is tantamount to death. They decide to sell him for a profit to an uncertain future as a slave in a merchants' caravan (cf. Ex 21:16; Dt 24:7). The results for the brothers, however, are as bad as the problem they sought to resolve. In the place of jealousy for a brother, they must now live with deception for their father. Slaughtering a goat, they dip Joseph's coveted coat into the

---

[1] Westermann, "Die Joseph-Erzählung," pp 11–25.

animal's blood. And they allow the father, who gave Joseph the coat as a sign of his first love, to draw his own, terrible conclusion: "A wild animal has devoured him."

The narrator does not drop the brothers from his characterization hook with the successful execution of their plot, however. With masterful insight into psychological patterns associated with guilt, he paints a panic-stricken and disoriented group before a mysterious, foreign potentate who accuses them of a capital crime. Rather than turning to each other at a time of crisis, each one turns on his brother with accusations that seek to lay the blame for their plight on his opposite number. Yet, even in the face of their anxiety, they open a new life of deception. When they report to their father that the mysterious ruler in Egypt wants to see the youngest son, the father accuses them of irresponsibility. They should not have told the man so much about the family (Gen 43:6). The brothers respond by telling the father that the man had elicited the information through specific questions. But no questions like that appear in the course of their interview with Joseph. Rather, they had fallen all over themselves to give the man all the information they could think of, information that might establish their innocence (Gen 42:13). Moreover, even at the point of reconciliation, the brothers remain under a quarrelsome burden (Gen 45:24). And a recapitulation of the denouement reports construction of a new alibi to provoke Joseph to an explicit assurance of forgiveness. The brothers tell Joseph that before their father died, he had asked them to ask Joseph for pardon for their misdeed (Gen 50:16-17). Joseph was unfortunately not present at this alleged final request, not in the primary structure of the story, not in the recapitulation. And to suppose that a section of the text with that missing scene has simply fallen out of our present material violates the description of relationships. The text as it now stands implies to the contrary that the brothers' allusion to the father's request was a ruse, an act of deception designed to secure Joseph's forgiveness without completely opening themselves to a relationship of trust (cf. also Gen 43:7). At the very end of the story, the brothers' ability to trust Joseph (and their own trustworthiness) does not appear to be any different than at the beginning of the story. If reconciliation is to occur for these brothers, it must occur without convincing evidence of changed character in the villains.

B. The father also contributed to the alienation. His preferential love for Joseph pinpointed the brothers' jealousy and hatred. He received Joseph's bad tales about the brothers (37:3). But to make matters worse, he demonstrated his love for the first-place son with a gift designed to symbolize Joseph's exalted position (37:3). And when the season for shepherding rolled around, he sent the group out. But Joseph? Joseph was a shepherd too (37:2). But Joseph remained at home, aloof from the work of the fields. It is little wonder, then, that the brothers hated Joseph. It is a surprise that they did not (openly) hate Jacob.

C. The chief burden of guilt for breaking the family and keeping it broken falls on Joseph himself, however, This point is more difficult to establish because Gen 39–41 paints the central hero as a saint, incapable of mistakes. When his master's wife tempts him, he rejects her advances, not simply because to accept would be a sin against God, but because to accept would violate the responsibility he owes to his master (39:8–9). When the Pharaoh's servants appeal to him for interpretation of dreams, he provides for each, even though one interpretation involves a death sentence (Gen 40). When the Pharaoh needs a dream interpreter, he responds with wisdom and perception, to find himself promoted to a position of power in the nation second only to the Pharaoh himself (41:39). In every case he is the paragon of a skilled administrator, concerned for his master, concerned for his people.[2]

Gen 39–41 may present Joseph as a figure of legendary virtue. But the remaining sections of the Joseph story mince no words in describing the opposite side of his character. In Gen 37 this point is not difficult to see. Joseph is the spoiled child, pampered by his father, insensitive to his brothers' feelings about him. Thus, he brings bad stories about the brothers to the father. He receives a coat from the father to designate his exalted position and even wears that coat when he goes to inquire about his brothers' well-being. He dreams grandiose dreams and freely flaunts them and their obvious significance to all members of the family.

Joseph's peculiar brand of love and concern for his family does not stop, however, with his immature display of disdain at home. When the brothers come to buy grain in Egypt, Joseph recognizes them immediately and treats them harshly. He accuses them of spying, a charge as cruel and false as Potiphar's wife's accusation in Gen 39. He leaves Simeon sitting in prison for two years, just as the cup-bearer had left Joseph sitting in prison until circumstances required a new course of events. He hides money in the food bags, opening the brothers' fear that they would be accused of theft as well as spying. And the final blow: He hides a silver cup in Benjamin's bag and confronts the brothers with a threat to detain Benjamin in Egypt. Charles Fritsch defends the positive character of Joseph, even at this point in the story. It is somewhat unexpected, then, that one of his observations picks up the point quite effectively: "One can still sense the feeling of unbridled, *ruthless* power in the action of Joseph as he lords it over his cowering fearful brethren, and plays with them as a cat plays with a mouse. They are entirely at his mercy, and he can do anything he wants to them."[3] Fritsch concludes that despite the show of despotic unconcern for the brothers, Joseph reveals a true character that is more positive. That ideal character, according to Fritsch, is expressed in Joseph's concern for Benjamin and his old father. But this conclusion misses the thrust of the story. The alienation

---

[2] So, Coats, "The Joseph Story . . . ," pp. 285–297.
[3] Fritsch, pp. 27–28. Italics added here.

in the family is not between Joseph and Benjamin. It does not concern the relationship between Joseph and his overprotective father. It zeroes in on Joseph and the brothers. And in that relationship Fritsch is correct. Joseph displays a despotic unconcern for his prey, an unconcern that continues to the very height of the denouement in Gen 45.

Joseph's character is even more devious than Fritsch suggests, however. It would be bad enough for the brothers if they knew the dangers of presenting themselves so vulnerably before the victim they had kidnapped years earlier. Then they could understand the severity of their plight. But they did not know. The text repeats the note that Joseph recognized his brothers but they did not recognize him. Thus they were forced to interpret their plight as a terrible fate, the punishment of God, or simply as a mystery that remained beyond them. They were like chaff tossed about by a haphazard wind, moved without sense. And at the opposite pole, Joseph's despotic power carries the increased threat of cold, impersonal anonymity.

At the crux of the denouement, then, the Joseph story leaves its audience with a pressing question: How can people who have no merit for reconciliation present themselves to each other as candidates for a restored relationship? The problem is even more severe: The principals in the Joseph story do not claim reconciliation as a restored relationship imposed by the innocent party on the guilty parties, imposed as it were from above. They make no pretenses for such holiness. Joseph requires no ritual of repentance from the brothers for their past sins. He requires no evidence of changed character in the brothers to guarantee the sanctity of the present relationship. The brothers lay no claim for extenuating circumstances provoking the initial violation of Joseph. They ask no mercy. They offer no apologies. They require no apologies from Joseph. Indeed, one has the impression that if reconciliation in the Joseph story must wait for guarantees that the people involved will never act so much like people again, it will never occur. Significantly, then, the brothers' recognition of their guilt before Joseph, their "confession" as it were, occurs *before* they know who Joseph is. After they know, no such recognition and confession appear. Such unconscious confession, such absence of conscious confession can hardly signal a moral awakening. S. R. Driver misses the importance of this point. He argues that Joseph uses his advantage over his brothers "to *try* them, to discover whether they are loyal to his father and youngest brother, and then, when he has at last assured himself of their altered mind . . . , when he is satisfied, in other words, that they are *worthy* to be forgiven, he discloses himself to them and nobly and magnanimously forgives them."[4] But nothing could be farther from the case. Not only do the brothers as a group do nothing as a group to show that they were all willing to go into slavery for the sake of

---

[4] S. R. Driver, *The Book of Genesis* (*Westminster Commentaries,* 2nd ed; London: Methuen, 1904) 320.

their father and youngest brother, but there is also no absolution from Joseph that would mark a noble and magnanimous act of forgiveness. The restored relationship does not depend on a mutually accepted attitude toward the past, but a workable attitude toward the future. It is that movement that signals a moral awakening among the members of this family tragedy. At the point of the denouement, then, the plot sets the faces of the warring parties toward the future. And it requires a mutual commitment for survival in the face of a common crisis.

The character of that commitment, then, is crucial for the reconciliation of the family. It involves all members of the family who share in the responsibility for the alienation. The following paragraphs are designed to explore that commitment.

1. Commitment is not an easy matter. Judah is the first to demonstrate the threat it poses. Challenged by the prospects of perpetual enslavement for Benjamin and the dire consequences that enslavement would produce for his father (as well as for himself), he offers himself in Banjamin's place. He had sworn an oath to his father to bring Benjamin home safely. He had shared in a rash oath to Joseph's servants to condemn to death any person whose equipment concealed the silver cup. What else could he do? Stripped of his defenses, he could only step forward, alone, and make his offer. And in his offer, the entire scope of his future was radically altered. "Now therefore let your servant, I pray you, remain instead of the lad as a slave to my lord; and let the lad go back with his brothers."

Judah's move opened the door to a new future for the brothers. One should not over-idealize the commitment, however. He had no real choice. One wonders, had the circumstances been different, whether Judah could have committed himself to that kind of future. But it was precisely the circumstances of the occasion, not Joseph's loving care, or a prior moral awakening, or an essential element of Judah's character, that provoked the commitment. And Judah responded. Perhaps the threat of that kind of commitment is not its requirements for a future of slavery, but its requirements for a complete uncovered, unprotected self-revelation. It offers no place to hide, no means for controlling the future. The intimacy would be overwhelming.

2. Jacob also confronted a mysterious fate, a requirement for commitment. When one has no food and no chance for getting food, he has no real future, no choice. Thus, Jacob committed his most prized possession, his key for the future—Benjamin (cf. Gen 22). Moreover, the fate that seemed to control the future of Jacob's family haunted Jacob with a conviction that Benjamin, like Joseph, would never return (cf. Gen 43:14b). Yet, in the face of apparent hopelessness Jacob blesses his sons in the journey. And the goal of the blessing is not simply the successful purchase of food. It is for the safe return of "your other brother and Benjamin." The hopeless man hopes. He hopes for Simeon, a prisoner for two years, and for Benjamin. But even in

his mysterious hope despite a haunting fate, his hope for his sons, one glimpses the scope of the story's full denouement. A hope rooted in God, indeed, in God's promises for full posterity, undergirds the movement toward Egypt. *(We get few things in God's eye. It may seems hopeless to our eyes but hopeful to God's eye.)*

Then comes the good news. Joseph is not dead. He is alive. No explanation about past deception is necessary between Jacob and his other sons. Perhaps the bloody robe was forgotten in the joy of the good news. Perhaps Jacob knew all along. But in either case, it did not make any difference. Explanations are not in order when one is overcome with the joy of a resurrection. But there is more. Joseph's resurrection means a sudden unexpected prospect for reconciliation.

It is not easy for an old man to move to a new country. It requires cutting ties, burning bridges. It requires a new kind of commitment, a commitment without protection. But Jacob committed himself anyway, his life, his family, his reconciliation with his sons, the promise to produce a great nation. He had no disguise, no façade, no escape. Perhaps the threat of that kind of commitment is not its requirement to believe lying sons, but its requirement for a movement into the future without reservations, without alternative directions, without a proper control over the circumstances. It would require a complete, unprotected intimacy.

3. Joseph also committed himself. And perhaps his was the most dangerous commitment of all. Joseph had power. And he had protection. Moreover, his protection had the advantage of anonymity, the opposite of a threatening intimacy. But Joseph stripped himself. He revealed himself to his brothers. He could no longer act the role of the mysterious, powerful potentate of Egypt. Now he would be the son of Jacob, the lord of the dreams. But would such a self-revelation not be relatively safe? After all, he did not forfeit his power. Yet, that is just the point of commitment. When a man in power reveals his secrets to potential opposition, he lays his power on the line. Joseph had had power in Jacob's family. And those very same brothers had stabbed him in the back. Might they not do it again? Joseph had no guarantees. He requested none. He requested no rituals of repentance and atonement. Rather, he ran the risk of intimate commitment with the promise to provide for those brothers and Jacob within the context of the Pharaoh's court.

Yet, one might object, did Joseph not secure his revenge before the reconciliation occurred? An eye for an eye. A tooth for a tooth. And so each violation Joseph sets on his brothers' backs parallels the violation Joseph himself endured from the brothers' hands. There is just punishment for sin. Atonement ritual dances before the reader's eyes even though the brothers who share the strange minuet do not know that the blood bath they face threatens from the hands of their offended victim. Revenge may well characterize properly the process of Joseph's trial with his victims. Yet, it seems to me to be crucial that the reconciliation does not orient toward the past, toward the violations or revenge as just payment for the violations. It orients toward the future. A famine is at hand. And the brothers need each other in spite of themselves.

Thus, reconciliation for Jacob's family lies in the future, a dangerous future, a future built on mutual commitment among people who have already shown their true colors. Who knows? Perhaps Joseph would try to execute his brothers for spying after all. Perhaps the brothers would continue their scheming and deception. Perhaps the father would find new ways to express his oppressive preference for Joseph. Living in reconciliation with people like that, with no guarantees to control future relationships, threatens life and limb.[5]

There is a refreshing kind of affirmation about the possibilities for human life in the Joseph story. The author does not try to disguise the all too human characteristics of his principals, the pride and jealousy, the guilt and hopelessness, the anxiety and desperate trust. But in the middle of all this humanity lies a future, a workable future. That future depends on the human skill and commitment of the reconciled partners, each ready to risk what he has to support his brothers. And behind the risk is God's leadership, pointing his people to a future with promise. It is a future with a great posterity and a great land. It is a future with a blessing for all the nations of the earth. To that future the risk of reconciliation in a naked, intimate relationship with fallible, corrupt brothers is worthwhile.

II. POLITICAL POWER

The major plot in the Joseph story turns on tensions within a family. It moves from the tragic disposal of an obnoxious brother and deception of the father through the deceptive scheme of the disposed brother to final reconciliation and reunion of the family. In addition to the basic plot, the story develops a major sub-plot, Gen 39–41. In order to explore the breadth of the Joseph story adequately, one cannot overlook the distinctive goals of the political legend.

The sub-plot opens with the handsome Joseph confronted by the seductive demands of his master's wife. Joseph's stoic rejection of the woman's invitation exemplifies the admonitions of the wise men to avoid a woman whose husband is away from home (Prov 6:20–35; 7:10–27).[6] But the intention of the legend is not to emphasize the hero's rejection of a loose woman. In the second scene, Joseph responds to the despondency of his two

---

[5] Cf. also S. T. Kimbrough, "Reconciliation in the Old Testament," *Religion in Life* 41 (1972) 37–45. Kimbrough makes a similar point by noting that reconciliation does not depend on final resolution of tensions within a given community, but rather on the solidarity, the mutual commitment of the community in spite of internal tensions.

[6] So, von Rad, "Ancient Wisdom . . . ," p. 295.

new masters by interpreting their dreams. His perception exemplifies the skill of the wise dream interpreters at home in royal courts (cf. Dan 1:17–20; 2:12; 4:18). To be sure, he can interpret dreams because God gives him insight (cf. Gen 41:39). But the divine element does not override his skill, his god-given wisdom. Yet, the principal thrust of the sub-plot does not lie in Joseph's ability to interpret dreams. In both scenes, Joseph's rejection of a loose woman and his perception for interpreting dreams point beyond the limits of the scene to the final stage of the sub-plot. In the final scene, Joseph again interprets dreams. But the scene does not dwell on his ability to interpret. Joseph counsels the Pharaoh to order his kingdom in a particular way. But the scene does not emphasize the hero's ability to speak in a carefully constructed manner at crucial points. In each scene, Joseph rises from a low state to a position of power. But the principal intention of the legend is not to illustrate the proper way for a young man to rise to a position of power in the court. Rather, the legend focuses on the proper use of power by an administrator already in office.

Thus, Joseph rejects the advances of his master's wife, not only because fools fall into such traps. He rejects the woman because responsible administration of his office demands that he not violate the trust of his master. He interprets the dreams of the Pharaoh's baker and cup-bearer, not simply because dream interpretations come from God and deserve to be announced. He interprets their dreams because his office demands responsible, perceptive explanation of the visions his masters see. In the final scene, he gains an office of power because his perception and wisdom have demonstrated that he can administer the office responsibly.

An administrator in power should execute his office in the trust of his superior. This is perhaps the thrust of the temptress episode. But the same air of trust can be seen in the other scenes as well, both trust relationship with a superior and trust relationship with the people generally (cf. 41:56–57). The wise administrator must also carry out his office in a way that commands the trust and respect of the people. Without their support, he has no power (cf. Prov 14:28: "In a multitude of people is the glory of a king, but without people a prince is ruined.") Significantly, the people do not have a structure for expressing or denying their support. They must depend on the wise instruction, the education that brought the administrator to his office of power.

Yet, despite the absence of structures for a formal appeal for a judicial decision, except to a higher, more autocratic figure, the power figure who conforms to the wise ideal recognizes the importance of preserving the trust of the people. If his people place a trust in him, they should be able to depend on him to carry out that trust. That means that he cannot make his decisions under the influence of bribes from one faction or the other (Prov 17:8; 29:4). His administration must reflect justice (Prov 16:10,12; 29:14). He cannot prostitute his office to a personal vendetta, an effort to seek revenge against his foe (Prov 16:7; 24:17-18,28-29; 25:7b-10; 29:12). To do so would be to present the image of a spoiled child, pouting over wounded pride. He cannot let his tongue fly unbridled with the first thing that comes to mind (Prov 10:19; 11:12; 15:2; 17:27-28; 29:20). But of even more importance, his words must be straight. He does not tell his people what they want to hear, just to keep them quiet while he moves in some other direction according to his own whim (Prov 8:4-11; 16:13). There is no room among wise power figures for a Machiavellian prince.

In Gen 39-41 Joseph is the exemplar of the ideal. His responsibility is to rule his master's house within his master's trust. And that he does in all matters including his master's unfaithful wife. His responsibility is to rule the prison, to maintain the confidence of his subjects or his masters by just administration of his office. And that he does, even to the point of interpreting a dream for one of the Pharaoh's servants despite its death sentence. His responsibility to the Pharaoh is to gather grain from Egypt in anticipation of a famine, and then to administer the grain justly to all people. And that he does, not only for the Egyptians, but for the world (cf. Prov 11:26).

One of the striking products of careful construction in the Joseph story is a contrast between this ideal, legendary Joseph and the impulsive, rather cruel Joseph in Gen 37 and especially in chs. 42-44. In 42-44 Joseph is still in a position of political power. But his administration contradicts the wise and perceptive reign described in ch. 41. He does not present a trustworthy image. He speaks. But his words do not make sense. "You are spies." But they are not spies. The words can be manipulated by the politician to achieve his goals. And his goals outweigh all other ends (cf. Gen 47:13-26). In his position with absolute power over his brothers, as Machiavellian prince free to deceive when it fits his purposes, he moves his brothers like pawns on a chess board (cf. Prov 26:18f). There is no commitment, no reconciliation, no healing (cf. Prov 12:18). Where is the wise and perceptive administrator now? Thus, Joseph offers no sign of reconciliation until circumstances enable a change. He offers no recognition. There can be no intimacy. To the contrary, he must protect his position. He must act the role of a power politician. That means protecting himself from his former opponents, his brothers. That means keeping them on the defensive, not certain about the meaning of current events. That means deception. Reconciliation works against that position. To remove the disguise, to reveal identity, to commit to brothers without guarantee of their submission, that is not the role of a politician concerned to maintain his office of power. That is the concern of a reconciler. And a reconciler stands in a vulnerable position.

When Joseph reveals himself to his brothers, he is no longer acting like a politician whose principal concern is to defend his power. He cannot continue moving these men at his discretion. They are no longer pawns in a game. They are brothers. A man in a position of political power can use his power in the service of a brother. But he can also use a brother to maintain his power. A reconciler has a disadvantage. He cannot use his brothers. He must be devoted to them. Thus, the model of a reconciler is a wise man who brings healing with his tongue, not sword thrusts (Prov 12:18), not deception (Prov 26:18-19). The model is a servant who forfeits his own defenses, perhaps the chances to maintain his position of power, and even his own life, for the sake of his brother.

III. THE JOSEPH STORY AND ITS THEOLOGICAL CONTEXT

The two principal goals in the plot of the Joseph story, to describe reconciliation in a broken family despite the lack of merit among any of its members and to depict the characteristics of an ideal administrator, have theological roots. In depicting Joseph as an ideal power figure, the digression never makes its theological rootage a central feature. Joseph rejects Potiphar's wife, for example, not primarily because to accept would be a sin against God. The reference to God in Joseph's speech is not a part of the reason for rejecting the woman's invitation. There is no theological moralism here. There is a kind of human enlightenment, a commitment to a fellow man because he is a fellow who trusts the relationship, commitment to a relationship because only in that relationship does life make sense. Yet, the theological rootage is there, behind the scene. To violate trust with a master is equal to a sin against God.

The rootage is made clear at the beginning of each of the first two scenes. Joseph rises to a position of power not only because of his skill, but also because of God's presence. God does not intervene in the course of Joseph's affairs. Joseph rises to his positions of power because of his ability to administer the office. But God is nevertheless there. Does this kind of theological rootage mean that for the Joseph story man is only a puppet on a string?[7] He appears to work within the realm of normal affairs, free to rise by his own ability, or fall by his own failures. But in reality the God behind the scenes pulls all the strings. Joseph could, in reality, not fail to gain his position because God was with him. The logical implications of the assistance formulas in 39:2 and 23 might be pressed to such a conclusion. To evaluate this point, however, one must keep a broader scope of Old Testament theology in view. The assistance formula is a common element in the Old Testament.[8] A classic example of its use appears in Ex 3:11-17. Moses objects that he cannot execute the commission laid on his shoulders (vs. 11). But God responds with a promise for his presence (vs. 12). Indeed, the discussion about God's name in the following verses (vss. 13-15) connects the name, Yahweh, with the promise for presence. It is as if God

---

[7] So, Redford, p. 74.
[8] Cf. H. D. Preuss, ". . . ich will mit dir sein!" *ZAW* 70 (1968) 139-173.

says: "My very name is a symbol, a guarantee for my presence with you while you execute this commission."[9] On the basis of that promise, then, God repeats the commission (vss. 16–17). But one cannot conclude that Moses is only an automaton, dancing on the strings pulled by a great puppeteer in the sky. There is no basis for an Old Testament docetism here. Moses remains a free man, faced with problems resolvable only by his own skill. The promise for presence guarantees no more for Joseph than the Emmanuel child does for Ahaz, than the name does for Moses.

The problem continues with Joseph's confession that his ability to interpret dreams derives finally from God (40:8; 41:16,25). But to see Joseph as a puppet whose mouth moves while the ventriloquist speaks the words violates Israel's understanding of both God and man. Wisdom tradition provides perhaps the best context for interpreting the point. A wise man knows that he is responsible for his words. If his counsel fails, then he, not God, not the king, stands liable (cf. 2 Sam 17:23). Thus, the Proverbs counsel a man to avoid devious talk (Prov 4:24), to seek wisdom as a means for ordering a responsible life (Prov 8:4–21). But the wise man, trained to use his insight as a means for counsel, knows that to rely on his own insight alone is foolish: "Trust in the Lord with all your heart, and do not rely on your own insight. . . ." (Prov 3:5). The wise man cannot afford to think of himself as an automaton, to assume that his words come only from God as if he had no responsibility for their content. But neither can he afford to assume that his words come only from his own insight. The two poles must be held in tension. The same tension applies for Joseph's rise to power under the presence of God. The same tension applies for Ahaz's plight with Isaish and the kings of Samaria and Damascus. The same tension applies for Moses.

Joseph's self-revelation speech, 45:4–13, also has a theological rootage. Joseph explains three times (the repetition shows a crucial focus in the structure of the speech on this point, not evidence for literary expansions) that God, not the brothers, sent him to Egypt. This explanation should not be devalued as a sign of human slavery to a predestination designed by a puppeteering God. To be sure, it places the responsibility for the tragedy that broke the family apart on God. "It was not you who sent me here, but God." But the weight of the explanation does not lie in a justification of the past event. It does not intend to say that God pulled the string for the brothers' plot against Joseph. To the contrary, the weight of the explanation lies in the relationship of all those past tragedies to the coming event. "God sent me before you *in order to preserve a remnant on earth for you.*" The explanation is valid only as a new order emerges from the tragedy the

[9] Cf. Martin Buber, *Moses; The Revelation and the Covenant* (New York: Harper, 1958) 39–55.

brothers foisted onto Joseph. And that new, emerging order is possible because God creates the conditions that can support it, despite the violations of the past. The explanation thus implies no more, but also no less than the span of tension between promise and fulfillment, so characteristic for the entire Pentateuch. Indeed, the point ties directly with the promise to the patriarchs for a great progeny. Joseph makes the point explicitly that God sent him to Egypt in order to preserve "many survivors" for his family. The same speech has a second point, also with a theological ground. "God has made me lord of all Egypt." The best context for interpreting the point, as it seems to me, is the Pentateuchal gap between patriarchs and exodus, between Canaan and Egypt. The point is that because God enabled Joseph to become lord of Egypt, Jacob and all of his children can live despite the famine. They can move from the famine of Canaan to the source of life in Egypt. And it is in the move, the commitment of faith that enables the move, that reconciliation crowns the scene. This point cannot be shelved as a secondary addition to the speech. Prefigured by Joseph's dream and subsequently by his deportation, that move, that reconciliation, is the substance of the story.

The little unit of tradition in 46:1–7 was not an original part of the Joseph story. Yet, despite its secondary character, it makes a crucial contribution to the theology of this masterpiece. Its function is to comment on precisely the points of theology effectively expressed at the height of the story's climax in 45:4–13. The unit is cast as a theophany. In typical fashion God arrests Jacob's attention with a direct address: "Jacob, Jacob." And Jacob responds: "Here am I" (cf. Ex 3:4). God's speech then begins with a self-revelation formula. And the self-revelation attaches the Joseph story explicitly to the patriarchal traditions: "I am God, the God of your father" (cf. Ex 3:6). The speech itself focuses on Jacob's descent into Egypt: "Do not be afraid to go down to Egypt." And the reason is clear. In Egypt the promise for great progeny, so long delayed, will finally be fulfilled: "Because I will make you a great nation there." But along with the promise for his presence for the trip to Egypt, God also guarantees to bring Jacob back, an allusion to the exodus. In this commentary, Jacob's move to Egypt functions as a preparation for the exodus as well as a fulfillment of the promise for progeny. It demonstrates God's leadership for his people. It secures a reunion of Jacob's family. Can Jacob's move to Egypt in the body of the Joseph story itself be viewed as anything less?

The Joseph story ends with a report about Jacob's successful settlement in Goshen. History threatened Jacob with a tragedy. His family was broken apart. Now the family has been healed. The past was a curse. The present appears full of unexpected blessing. In keeping with the commission given to Abraham (12:1–3), Jacob blesses the Pharaoh. But what now? Jacob is fully acquainted with the threat of the future. Had he not thought his son lost? Had he not now left the security of Canaan with only a promise that he, or better, his descendants would return? His future would lie in Joseph's hands by God's promise. And there Jacob could find peace. But what about the future for Jacob's survivors?

The Joseph story is not primarily about Israel. The Pentateuch has stories about the people of God. The Joseph story is about Jacob, Joseph, and the brothers. It is difficult to say that the Joseph story reflects early history among the tribes of Israel. To seek some sign for the demise of Reuben or Simeon as tribes is to seek a sign that does not appear here. But the great survivors mentioned in Joseph's speech are Israel. The brothers are the ancestors for the tribes. Jacob is Israel. And the move to Egypt sets the stage for the sons of Jacob to become the Israelites, ready for the exodus. It is no accident, then, that the conclusion in 47:27 employs the name Israel. And the name suggests that the subject of the story is not simply a family.

But would the story of Joseph not describe the experiences of Israel as a people? A family broken by internal struggles. A family in search of reconciliation, not only in the wake of the exile, but from the beginning of her life as a people. A family at war with each other. A family reconciled under the personal authority of a man of power. A family with no internal merit for reconciliation. A family with no guarantees that warring will never break out again. A family at odds with each other despite the appearance of reconciliation. A family committed to each other and to their God despite their divisions. The Joseph story is a part of Israel's historical tradition. For the sons of Jacob the future holds a blessing: a great nation, a great land. What could they know of the Assyrians or the Babylonians? Yet, would it make any difference? For the sons of Israel the future means fulfilled promise, despite the famine of the present, despite deception and apparent hopelessness, despite life in a foreign land, despite continuing struggles with the family. The future can never be judged by the appearance of a curse in the present. The future must always be judged by the promise of blessing from the past, by the name of God in the present. For the Joseph story, that judgment opens the door to a new period of hope. First Joseph, then Benjamin, finally Jacob descend from Canaan to Egypt. They leave the land. But they shall return. The descent is, in a manner, descent into Sheol. But they shall return. From death to life. From Egypt to Canaan.

BIBLIOGRAPHY

N.B. Many relevant works of a more general nature, even though cited in the preceding pages, are omitted from this bibliography.

Abrahams, I. "Joseph's Coat of Many Colours," *ExpT* 20 (1909) 90.

Adock, N. "Genesis 41, 40b," *ExpT* 67 (1956) 383.

Ahuvyah, A. "Alle, die nach Aegypten kamen (Gen. 46.8-27)," *Bet Miqra'* 12 (1966/67) 119-122.

Albright, W. F. "Historical and Mythical Elements in the Story of Joseph," *JBL* 37 (1918) 111-143.

Anbar, M. "Changement des noms des tribus nomades dans la relation d'un même événement," *Bib* 49 (1968) 221-232.

Arenhoevel, D. "Die Gestalt des Joseph in der Überlieferung des AT'," *BK* 21 (1966) 8-10.

Argyle, A. W. "Joseph the Patriarch in Patristic Teaching," *ExpT* 67 (1955) 199-201.

Atir, E. "Zur Frage der Beziehung zwischen der biblischen Joseferzählung und der ägyptischen Brüdererzählung," *Bet Miqra'* 11 (1965/66) 3-8.

Bernhardt, K. H. "Anmerkungen zur Interpretation des KRT Textes von Ras Schamra-Ugarit," *Wissenschaftliche Zeitschrift der Ernst-Moritz-Arndt Universität* (Greifswald) 5 (1955/56) 101-121.

Brand, J. "The Title אשר על הבית ," *Tarbiz* 36 (1966/67) 221-228.

Brueggemann, W. "Life and Death in Tenth Century Israel," *JAAR* 40 (1972) 96-109.

Coats, George W. "The Joseph Story and Ancient Wisdom: A Reappraisal," *CBQ* 35 (1973) 285-297.

_____. "Redactional Unity in Genesis 37-50," *JBL* 93 (1974) 15-21.

Crenshaw, J. L. "Method in Determining Wisdom Influence upon 'Historical' Literature," *JBL* 88 (1969) 129-142.

Croatto, J. S. "*'Abrek,* 'Intendant' dans Gén XLI, 41, 43," *VT* 16 (1966) 113-115.

Cunen, F. "Les pratiques divinatoires attribuées à Joseph d'Egypte," *RevScRel* 33 (1959) 396-404.

Daube, David. "Law in the Narratives," *Studies in Biblical Law.* New York: *KTAV,* 1969, 3-10.

Driver, G. R. "Two Problems in the Old Testament Examined in the Light of Assyriology," *Syria* 33 (1956) 70-78.

Ehrlich, E. L. *Der Traum im alten Testament, BZAW* 73. Berlin: Töpelmann, 1953.

Eisler, R. "Der bunte Rock Josephs," *OLZ* 11 (1908) 368-371.

Engelbach, R. "The Egyptian Name of Joseph," *JEA* 10 (1924) 204-206.

Fritsch, Charles T. "God was with Him: A Theological Study of the Joseph Narrative," *Int* 9 (1955) 21-34.

Gan, M. "The Book of Esther in the Light of the Story of Joseph in Egypt," *Tarbiz* 31 (1961) 144–149.

Gressmann, H. "Ursprung und Entwicklung der Joseph-Sage," *FRLANT* 36. Göttingen: Vandenhoeck und Ruprecht, 1923, 1–55.

Gunkel, H. "Die Komposition der Joseph-Geschichten," *ZDMG* 76 (1922) 55–71.

——————. *Genesis übersetzt und erklärt,* 6 aufl. Göttingen: Vandenhoeck & Ruprecht, 1964.

Hals, Ron. *The Theology of the Book of Ruth. Facet Books, Biblical Series* 23; Philadelphia: Fortress, 1969.

Heaton, E. W. "The Joseph Saga," *ExpT* 59 (1947–48) 134–136.

Herrmann, S. "Joseph in Ägypten. Ein Wort zu J. Vergotes Buch 'Joseph en Egypte'," *TLZ* 85 (1960) 827–830.

Honeyman, A. M. "The Occasion of Joseph's Temptation," *VT* 2 (1952) 85–87.

Humphreys, W. Lee. *The Motif of the Wise Courtier in the Old Testament.* Dissertation. New York: Union, 1970.

Janssen, J. "Egyptological Remarks on the Story of Joseph in Genesis," *JEOL* 14 (1955/56) 63–72.

Joüon, P. "Locutions hébraïques: 6. Gen 44, 17," *Bib* 3 (1922) 59–61.

Kaiser, O. "Stammesgeschichtliche Hintergründe der Josephsgeschichte," *VT* 10 (1960) 1–15.

Kessler, Rainer. *Die Querverweise im Pentateuch. Überlieferungsgeschichtliche Untersuchung der expliziten Querverbindungen innerhalb des vorpriesterlichen Pentateuchs.* Dissertation, Heidelberg, 1972.

Kimbrough, S. T. "Reconciliation in the Old Testament," *Religion in Life* 41 (1972) 37–45.

Kingsbury, E. C. "He Set Ephraim Before Manasseh" *HUCA* 28 (1967) 129–136.

Kitchen, K. A. "The Term *Nšq* in Genesis XLI, 40," *ExpT* 69 (1957) 30.

Maigret, Jacques. "L'Histoire de Joseph," *BTS* 53–54 (1963) 2–4.

Margoliouth, D. S. "Gen 37, 28," *ExpT* 33 (1924) 39–40.

Martin-Achard, R. "Problèmes soulevés par l'étude de l'histoire biblique de Joseph," *RTP* 21 (1972) 94–102.

May, H. G. "The Evolution of the Joseph Story," *AJSL* 47 (1930/31) 83–93.

McEvenue, Sean E. *The Narrative Style of the Priestly Writer (An Bib* 50) Rome: Biblical Institute Press, 1971.

Meinhold, P. "Die Geschichte des Sinuhe und die alttestamentliche Diasporanovelle," *Wissenschaftliche Zeitschrift der Ernst-Moritz-Arndt Universität* (Greifswald) 20 (1971) 277–281.

Merwe, B. J. van der. "Joseph as Successor of Jacob," in *Studia Biblica et Semitica* (Wageningen: Veenman, 1966) 221–232.

Mettinger, Tryggve N. D. *Solomonic State Officials. A Study of the Civil Government Officials of the Israelite Monarchy* (Coniectanea Biblica; OT Series 5) Lund: Gleerups, 1971.

Morenz, Siegfried. "Joseph in Ägypten," *TLZ* 84 (1959) 401–416.

Murtagh, J. "The Egyptian Colouring of Genesis and Exodus," *Irish Ecclesiastical Record* 107 (1960) 2537-2560.

Naville, E. "The Egyptian Name of Joseph," *JEA* 12 (1926) 16-18.

Nestle, Eb. "Genesis XLV 23," *ExpT* 22 (1911) 526.

Noth, Martin. *A History of Pentateuchal Tradition.* Tr. Bernhard W. Anderson; Englewood Cliffs: Prentice-Hall, 1972.

Orlinsky, H. "Critical notes on Gen. 39, 14.17, Jud 11.37," *JBL* 61 (1942) 87-97.

Peck, J. "Note on Genesis 37,2 and Joseph's Character," *ExpT* 82 (1970/71), 342.

von Rad, Gerhard. *Biblische Josephserzählung und Josephsroman.* München: Kaiser, 1965.

──────. *Genesis, A Commentary.* Revised edition. Philadelphia: Westminster, 1972.

──────. "The Joseph Narrative and Ancient Wisdom," *Problem of the Hexateuch and Other Essays.* Tr. E. W. T. Dicken; London: Oliver and Boyd, 1966, 292-300.

──────. *Die Josephsgeschichte.* (*Biblische Studien* 5) Neukirchen: Neukirchener Verlag, 1956.

Raeder, S. "Die Josephsgeschichte im Koran und im AT," *EvT* 26 (1966) 169-190.

Redford, D. B. "The 'Land of the Hebrews' in Gen XL, 15," *VT* 15 (1965) 529-532.

──────. *A Study of the Biblical Story of Joseph (Genesis 37-50)* (*VT Sup* 20) Leiden: Brill, 1970.

Richter, W. "Traum und Traumdeutung in AT. Ihre Form und Verwendung," *BZ* 7 (1963) 202-220.

Rowe, A. "The Famous Solar City of On," *PEQ* 94 (1962) 133-142.

Ruppert, L. "Göttliche und menschliche Handeln. Form und Inhalt der Josephsgeschichte," *BK* 21 (1966) 1-36.

──────. *Die Josephserzählung der Genesis. Ein Beitrag zur Theologie der Pentateuchquellen* (*StANT* 11) München: Kösel Verlag, 1965.

Ruprecht, E. "mlṭ/plṭ," *Theologisches Handwörterbuch zum Alten Testament*, ed. E. Jenni and C. Westermann. München: Kaiser, 1971/72.

Schulte, Hannelis. *Die Entstehung der Geschichtesschreibung im Alten Israel* (*BZAW* 128) Berlin: Töpelmann, 1972.

Seybold, Donald. "Paradox and Symmetry in the Joseph Narrative," *Literary Interpretations of Biblical Narratives,* eds. Kenneth R. R. Gros Louis, James S. Ackerman, Thayer S. Warshaw. Nashville: Abingdon, 1974, 59-73.

Shochat, E. "Political Motives in the Stories of the Patriarchs," *Tarbiz* 24 (1955) 252-267.

Speiser, E. A. *Genesis (Anchor Bible,* 1) Garden City, N.Y.: Doubleday, 1964.

Stricker, B. H. "Prison de Joseph," *AcOr* 19 (1942) 101-137.

Vergote, J. *Joseph en Égypte, Genèse chap. 37-50 à la Lumière des Études Égyptologiques Récentes.* (*Orientalia et Biblica Lovaniensia,* 3) Louvain: Publications Universitaires, 1959.

Volz, Paul and Rudolph, Wilhelm. *Der Elohist als Erzähler. Ein Irrweg der Pentateuchkritik?* (*BZAW* 63) Giessen: Töpelmann, 1933.

Ward, W. A. "The Egyptian Office of Joseph," *JSS* 5 (1960) 144–150.

——————. "Egyptian Titles in Genesis 39–50," *BS* 114 (1957) 40–59.

Weber, E. "Vorarbeiten zu einer Kunftigen Ausgabe der Genesis. B. Die Josephsage," *ZAW* 34 (1914) 199–218.

Westermann, Claus. "Die Joseph-Erzählung," (*Calwer Predigthilfen* 5) Stuttgart: Calwer, 1970, 45–118.

Whybray, R. N. "The Joseph Story and Pentateuchal Criticism," *VT* 18 (1968) 522–528.

Winnett, F. V. "Re-Examining the Foundations," *JBL* 84 (1965) 1–19.

Wolff, H. W. "The Kerygma of the Yahwist," *Int* 20 (1966) 131–158.

Wright, G. R. H. "Joseph's Grave under the Tree by the Omphalos at Shechem," *VT* 22 (1972) 476–486.

——————. "The Mythology of pre-Israelite Shechem," *VT* 20 (1970) 75–82.

Zimmerli, W. "Ich bin Jahwe," *Geschichte und Altes Testament,* ed. M. Noth (*Beiträge zur historischen Theologie* 16) Tübingen: J. C. B. Mohr (Paul Siebeck), 1953, 179–209.

INDEX OF MODERN AUTHORS

BIBLICAL INDEX